Poke

Hawai‘i's Food

Star★Advertiser

Books by Chef Sam Choy

Sam Choy's Cuisine Hawai'i
*Featuring the Premier Chefs
of the Aloha State*
(Pleasant Hawaii, Inc., 1990)

With Sam Choy
Cooking from the Heart (1995)

Sam Choy's Cooking
Island Cuisine at Its Best (1996)

The Choy of Seafood
Sam Choy's Pacific Harvest (1998)

Sam Choy's Kitchen
*Cooking Doesn't Get Any Easier
Than This* (1999)

Sam Choy's Poke
Hawai'i's Soul Food (1999)

Sam Choy's Island Flavors
*Cook Your Way to Paradise with
More Than 200 Delicious Recipes
from Hawai'i's Master Chef*
(Hyperion, 1999)

Sam Choy's Sampler
Hawai'i's Favorite Recipes (2000)

Sam Choy's Cooking with Kids
(2001)

Sam Choy Woks the Wok (2001)

Sam Choy's Polynesian Kitchen
*More Than 150 Authentic
Dishes from One of the World's
Most Delicious and
Overlooked Cuisines*
(Hyperion, 2002)

Sam Choy and the
Makaha Sons'
A Hawaiian Lū'au
*Recipes, Music, and
Talk Story* (2003)

Sam Choy's Little Hawaiian
Cookbook for Big Appetites (2003)

Sam Choy's Little Hawaiian
Poke Cookbook (2004)

Aloha Cuisine (2006)

Poke (2009)

Poke

Hawai'i's Food

Chef Sam Choy

PHOTOGRAPHY BY **Douglas Peebles**

FOOD STYLING BY **Karen Jones**

EDITING / WRITING BY **Cynthia Liu, Karen Lofstrom, Matthew Martin, and Curt Sanburn**

Mutual Publishing

Copyright © 2015 by Mutual Publishing
All rights reserved.

No part of this book may be reproduced in any form or by any electronic or mechanical means, including information storage and retrieval devices or systems, without prior written permission from the publisher, except that brief passages may be quoted for reviews.

All brand names and product names used in this book are trademarks, registered trademarks, or trademarks of their respective holders. Mutual Publishing, LLC is not associated with any product or vendor in this book.

All photography © Douglas Peebles, except (see below)
Photos © Sharmil Elliott: p. 112, 113
Photos © Ian Gillespie: p.xii (bottom), p. xiv (top), xviii, 1 (bottom)
Photos © Poke to the Max Documentary and Rea Pineda: p. xvi, xvii (top), p. 147-157 (background), 146-149, 150 (bottom), p. 151, 152 (top), 153
Photos by Kaz Tanabe: p. 66, 89, 111, 114, 117, 129

Photos from dreamstime.com:
Backgrounds:
p. i, ii, iv, vi, viii, x, xiv, 4, 7, 158-176 © Voyagerix; p. 27-30, 32, 34, 35, 36, 38-40, 42, 44, 45, 47, 49, 50 © Konstanttin; p. 53-55, 57, 58, 60, 61, 63- 66, 69, 71-74, 76, 77 © Archlombardo; p. 79, 80, 82-87, 89, 90, 92 © Smitea; p. 95, 97-103 © Artography; p. 105-111, 113-131 © Klikk; p. 133-145 © Loonger

Fish icon: © Cherverikoff; p. v (top) © Arnaud Weisser, (bottom) © Andrej Isakovic; p. vi (top) © Kalinin Dmitriy, (bottom) © Mchudo; p. vii (top) © Anonio Muñoz Palomares, (bottom) © Vasiu; p. viii (top) © Fedor Kondratenko, (bottom) © Barbro Bergfeldt; p. xiv (bottom) Vasiu; p. 3 (center) © Fedor Kundratenko; p. 8 (top) © Arnaud Weisser; p. 13 © Vitaly Vasin; p. 15 © Stanislav Dyudin; p. 17 (top) © Arnaud Weisser; p. 32 © Atman; p. 34 (top) © Shariff Che\' Lah; p. 36 © Arnaud Weisser; p. 38 © Norman Chan; p. 39 © Elena Moiseeva; p. 45 © Barbro Bergfeldt; p. 49 © Ruben Paz; p. 58 © Vasiu; p. 60 © Lukasz Olek; p. 63 © Edward Westmacott; p. 65 (top) © Le-thuy Do; p. 69 © David Coleman; p. 71 © Le-thuy Do; p. 72 © Maceofoto; p. 74 © Sally Scott; p. 77 © Yingthun; p. 80 © Peoplesmile; p. 82 © Elena Moiseeva; p. 84 © Tomboy2290; p. 85 © Casaalmare; p. 87 © Elena Elisseeva; p. 90 © Mchudo; p. 98 (top) © Vasiu; p. 99 © Atman; p. 101 © Andrej Isakovic; p. 108 © Vitalinar; p. 123 © Mchudo; p. 124 © Vasiu; p. 126 © Adisa; p. 135 © Iwka; p. 136 © Le-thuy Do; p. 138 © Angelo Gilardelli; p. 139 © Valentyn75; p. 140 © Angelo Gilardelli; p. 141 © Stuartbur; p. 142 © Chode; p. 143 © Sommail; p. 150 (top) © Iwka; p. 152 (bottom) © Mchudo; p. 154 © Edward Westmacott

ISBN-13: 978-1939487-48-3
Food photography art direction by Karen Jones

First Printing, October 2015
Second Printing, May 2016
Third Printing, February 2018
Fourth Printing, April 2021

Mutual Publishing, LLC
1215 Center Street, Suite 210
Honolulu, Hawai'i 96816
Ph: 808-732-1709 / Fax: 808-734-4094
email: info@mutualpublishing.com
www.mutualpublishing.com

Printed in South Korea

Contents

Calabash Cousins

Cooked Poke

Poke on the Road

Foreword

Poke (POE-kay) is Hawai'i's king of food, definitely its soul food. It is eaten everywhere—from potlucks to elegant get-togethers. It is on the menu of five-star dining rooms, plate lunch stands, sushi and izakaya restaurants, and even food trucks. And it is available wherever food is sold—supermarkets, wine shops, and warehouse clubs.

No one person is more synonymous with poke than Chef Sam Choy. He literally put poke back on the map in 1991 when he started his Poke Festival inviting chefs and anyone from the community to share their favorite poke recipes. That same year he opened his Kona restaurant on the Big Island serving poke with new and different ingredients and even offering it cooked—fried poke. Hawai'i's Regional Cuisine chefs picked up on poke's versatility adding their own touches, and today's chefs have developed even newer poke ways—poke bowls.

Today, poke is popular not just in Hawai'i but across the mainland, particularly where locals have moved or where there are chefs who have visited or cooked in the islands. This is not surprising. Poke is easy to make. It can be experimental, adding whatever is in the cupboard or fridge, or one's own favorite ingredients to the basics of shoyu, sesame oil, and chili pepper water. And it is a healthy food dish.

At the *Honolulu Star-Advertiser* we know of poke's popularity by feedback from readers of our Wednesday's Today Food section. Hawai'i's culinary scene and food traditions are an integral part of HSA's coverage of island lifestyle. By participating in this new edition of Sam's poke book, we want to share in the coverage of this delicious local food and Hawai'i's latest export to the world.

—Dennis Francis
President and Publisher,
Honolulu Star-Advertiser
and O'ahu Publications, Inc.

Preface

As the rest of the world is beginning to realize, the Pacific is the place for raw fish. The ultimate fresh food, with its delicate flavors and suave, inviting textures, it stars in dishes like ceviche from Peru, sashimi from Japan, poisson cru from Tahiti, kinilaw from the Philippines, and, gloriously, poke (POE-kay) from Hawai'i. When I wrote my book, *The Food of Paradise,* poke was one of the more fascinating and delicious dishes I encountered, a dish whose roots went back to the first Polynesians who came to the Islands.

In the twentieth century, poke went multicultural, absorbing influences from immigrants from across Asia who now called the Islands home. By the 1960s, it was entering Hawai'i's culinary mainstream, served as a pūpū in restaurants and bars. Now, poke is everywhere—in grocery stores and fish markets, in humble plate lunch places and in fancy restaurants not only in Hawai'i, but also in the continental U.S.

Sam Choy, immersed since childhood in the foods of the Islands, had the foresight to predict that Hawai'i's own raw fish dish could become an Island signature, as essential to Island identity as surfing and SPAM® musubi. In 1991, he and other innovative chefs organized the first poke contest. In this book, Sam invites readers to join him in exploring the possibilities of poke—the subtle variations of flavor and texture that result from different combinations of fish and seasonings.

The right condiments can bring raw fish to life: A touch of lime "cooks" ceviche, and wasabi and ginger highlight the delicacy of sashimi. Sam begins with the condiments of the ancient Hawaiians—the briny seaweeds they collected from the reefs, the sea salt they dried in the sun, and the kukui nuts they ground to a paste. Then he moves on to Asian flavors: sesame seeds, sesame oil, and chili pepper. If that weren't enough, he invites other chefs to share their ideas and recipes. So buy the freshest fish you can, call up some friends, crack open a few beers, and celebrate Hawai'i's gift to American cuisine.

—Rachel Laudan,
author of *The Food of Paradise*

Acknowledgments

To my beloved Carol—
always making sure the boat's on course and in tiptop shape.

And to Sam Jr., Chris, and Tini—
without you the voyage would be meaningless.

Just as a dish of appetizing poke requires mixing many good ingredients, a cookbook like this one requires the input, help, and effort of many people—editors, photographers, food stylists, chefs, designers, administrative assistants. I am indebted to the following individuals who helped make this book possible (I hope I haven't left anyone out!):

Richard Ahn, Keri Castillo, Somphet Chanpheng, Sharmil Elliot, Aurelio Garcia, Ian Gillespie, Jane Gillespie, Leo Gonzalez, Sandie Hata, Kyle Higa, Karen Jones, Mona Kwon, Jeffrey Lee, Cynthia Liu, Matthew Martin, Alfred Monico, John Patterson, Doug Peebles, Erika Roberts, Curt Sanburn, Dawn Sueoka, Brooks Takanaka, Kaz Tanabe, Elisa Tsukayama, Jesmer Victorino, Sally Watanabe Kim, Gay Wong, Eric Woo, Courtney Young

I would also like to thank my fellow chefs, who shared their recipes and their staff.

Chef Mark Ellman, Chef D. K. Kodama, Derek Kurisu, Chef Emeril Lagasse, Chef James McDonald, Chef Hideaki "Santa" Miyoshi, Chef Jeffrey Mora, Chef Tylun Pang, Chef Charles Phan, Chef Russell Siu, Mel Tanioka, Chef Alan Wong

I am especially grateful for Karen Lofstrom's excellent assistance in editing the recipes and organizing the book.

And finally, a big mahalo to Bennett Hymer for his continuing support.

Introduction

Chopped raw fish, or poke, was part of my everyday life growing up in Lā'ie, the rural town on O'ahu's north shore. The sea was our playground. As kids, we crawled around in the sand and tide pools; then we went further out to swim, surf, or fish. In my Hawaiian-Chinese 'ohana, there were several fishermen who helped out with baby sitting, so we kids found ourselves getting tangled in uncle's nets, napping inside canoes, and eating the fruits of the hukilau. Almost daily, when the fishermen returned to shore, they would quickly fillet a pāpio or an 'ō'io right on the spot, chop the flesh into chunks, add some limu and salt, and pass it around. As always, the food they prepared was shared, and the leftovers brought home for dinner or given to the neighbors. For us, poke was a staple food, a part of our daily lives.

And for many of us here in Hawai'i, it still is! According to the experts, poke has been eaten in the Islands longer than any other food. Captain James Cook was served a simple form of poke during his visits to Hawai'i in 1778 and 1779. Today, poke found everywhere. It is sold in wine stores, supermarkets and corner grocery stores. It is served at Island parties and celebrations, and

featured on the menus at hole-in-the-walls, izakayas, and five-star fine dining rooms. Like rubber slippers, "Eddie Would Go" bumper stickers, and the ability to eat peas with chopsticks, it is a reliable cue in the old game of "who's local." For me, poke is the king of Island foods.

According to the *Hawaiian Dictionary,* poke means "to slice, cut crosswise into pieces, as wood or fish," and is pronounced *POE-kay.* The term came to be used as shorthand for any sort of raw fish, gutted and gilled, and then sliced along the backbone. In the old days, the whole slice would be eaten, skin, bones, and all. Inedible portions were picked or spat out. When the raw fish was "prepared," it meant the fish was mashed (lomi), or other ingredients were added to it, mostly salt and savories like ʻopihi, lobster, sea urchin roe, kukui nut relish, and different kinds of limu (seaweed)—manauea, līpeʻepeʻe, kohu, līpoa, etc.

Since my formative years in Lāʻie, I've watched (and encouraged!) poke's evolution in Hawaiʻi. The first phase beyond its rootsy Hawaiian-ness occurred when Chinese and Japanese immigrants took to it. Fish was inexpensive back then, and many newcomers had fishing backgrounds of their own. A cultural appreciation for fresh raw fish helped the new immigrants make connections with their Hawaiian friends and co-workers. Asian poke-lovers added their own seasonings: shoyu, sesame seeds, green and white onions,

and hot peppers, to name a few. Their Hawaiian friends quickly adopted the new flavors.

Transformed in ways like this from its simple origins, modern poke became a quintessential local dish, a regular treat at a baby lūʻau, a beach party, or any get-together. Poke was easy to prepare, so if in a hurry and no time to cook, that was the dish to make and bring to a party. On Molokaʻi and other rural parts of the Islands, it was still the fishermen who made it and shared it with others. In Honolulu and other places, fresh poke began to show up in grocery stores and markets. Supermarket chains were selling prepared poke as early as 1973.

At about the time I was starting out as a chef, poke started to be served up in Honolulu hostess bars where the waitress or hostess would offer free pūpū, (mostly salty ones to get you to buy more drinks). In hindsight, it's easy to explain why: Poke didn't take up much kitchen space, and it was quick to prepare (and, of course, popular).

Early in my chef career, I made it my goal to have a locally rooted Hawaiian dish go mainstream. The Islands had already exported homegrown arts like the hula, surfing, and music—even aloha itself—but never a food. Sadly and unfairly, our staff of life, poi (the ʻono and nutritious mashed taro root), had become a punch line. Poke was the logical choice. While there are other unique dishes in the Islands, most have counterparts in other cuisines. Laulau are similar to Mexican tamales or Eastern-European cabbage rolls, and kālua pork is not too different from pulled pork.

To learn more, I researched similar raw-fish dishes in the South Pacific. On Rapa Nui and Pitcairn islands, the flesh of the aku is cut up and mixed with the innards and blood of the fish. There's the famous *poisson cru* of the Tuamotus and Tahiti, in which raw fish is "cooked" with lime juice. The Fijian preparation similar to poisson cru is called kokoda. Throughout Oceania, prepared raw reef fish is common.

By the early 1990s, a number of creative Island chefs, both professional and amateur, were improvising with basic poke, taking it to new levels. In 1991, have a venue to showcase their innovations, my friend Gene Egar and I launched the Sam Choy Poke Festival and Recipe Contest in Waimea on the Big Island. Our goal was to bring poke into the limelight. The festival attracted national food writers who couldn't resist a good reason to visit Hawai'i. And once they tasted poke, the publicity flowed. Now in its eighteenth year and held on O'ahu, the festival keeps generating innovative and delicious new ways to prepare poke.

In the late 90s, poke began showing up in cosmopolitan menus outside of Hawai'i. It was a natural: Poke lends itself easily to fantastic presentations that befit its noble Hawaiian background and its primal majesty. Even the

simplest poke dish can be displayed in a mouth-wateringly colorful palette. Poke was becoming Hawai'i's epicurean ambassador to the world.

When I'm cooking on the Mainland, poke is the dish most requested. It provokes the most audience participation and interest when I am speaking. (The constant question I get is how to pronounce it—the dish itself is so easily understood.) There are still times when I have to camouflage my poke for people squeamish about eating raw fish, but the worldwide popularity of Japanese sashimi and sushi has helped to overcome this obstacle.

In my first cookbook, *Sam Choy's Poke,* I highlighted entries from the poke festival. I called poke "Hawai'i's soul food," the dish we crave when we're away from the Islands for any length of time, the one we just don't feel right if we haven't had lately, the food we rely on to fill us up spiritually. Ten years later came *Poke by Chef Sam Choy and Friends* which covered the accelerating evolution of poke, showing how the original Polynesian poke has grown tall and flowered around the globe to surprise and delight all. This book, *Poke: Hawai'i's Food,* although with a slight name change, is more compact and affordable and more convenient to have in the kitchen, to send or take back to friends and families living on the mainland, or if you are a visitor to the islands, to bring back home for gift-giving.

The recipes come from my own designs, developed over the years. Some of them call for chopped tofu or vegetables instead of raw fish. And why not? Hawaiian culture is inclusive. Poke is also delicious over rice or noodles, tumbled into salads, folded into burritos and lumpia,

Introduction

molded into patties and loaves, and even flash-fried or lightly seared and served as a complete meal as poke bowls.

I have been helped by contributions from fellow chefs locally and abroad, who are also expanding the very definition of poke and spreading the Hawaiian food gospel. I am especially grateful that this collection includes recipes from Alan Wong, Emeril Lagasse, Mark Ellman, D. K. Kodama, James McDonald, Santa Miyoshi, Tylun Pang, Derek Kurisu, Charles Phan, Russell Siu, and Mel Tanioka. These guys honor poke in whole new ways.

As in all my cookbooks, I try to keep the recipes simple and let the reader operate within his or her own circle of flavors. I've added many flavor choices, reduced saltiness, and pared down the number of hard-to-get seasonings. Cooking should be fun and improvisational. The reader should be the ultimate creator, and a recipe shouldn't hinge on exotic ingredients or exact amounts. I can think of many elaborate sauces that would go well with poke, but they would detract from its essential simplicity.

Whether you want an appetizer that's inexpensive and easy to prepare or a fancy entrée that will wow your guests, there's something here for you. Enjoy!

A hui hou,

Sam Choy

How to Use This Book

I'm a minimalist when it comes to writing recipes for my cookbooks. My editors always want me to spell everything out, but my experience is that a detailed recipe can intimidate readers who usually have more common sense than editors give them credit for. I also find that home cooks like to add or subtract as well as improvise according to their circle of flavors. For this book I've done more spelling-out than usual, but maybe not enough to satisfy someone totally unfamiliar with poke.

If you're an experienced poke chef and know you like lots of chili peppers, or want to add some extra crunch with ogo and chopped cucumber, don't feel you have to follow these recipes to the letter. If the dish seems dry and you want to add a little more sauce, please do so. Restaurant chefs make these kinds of small adjustments all the time.

If you're new to this kind of cooking, follow the recipes closely the first time. That's the safest thing. Once you've made the dish and have a feeling for how it should look, or how you want it to taste, feel free to improvise. Recipes should be an inspiration, not a straitjacket.

A number of the poke recipes call for diced tomatoes. To keep it easy, none of the instructions call for seeding the tomatoes. However, if you believe that tomatoes should be seeded before they are diced, seed away.

I use Hawaiian chili peppers liberally. These small, thin, hot peppers are grown in backyards all over the Islands. When I prepare them for cooking, I leave the seeds inside as they are the source of the hotness of the peppers. I like the kick that HOT gives. But if you aren't all that fond of hot food and want to turn down the heat a little, seed the peppers before chopping or mincing them. In place of the Hawaiian chili peppers, you can use the small red Thai chilies or any Asian red chili peppers.

Good cooking starts with good shopping. Tasty local ingredients, or exactly the right condiments, can make all the difference.

Look for the best LOCAL produce in your area. No vegetable that comes from miles away is going to taste quite as sweet and fresh as one grown nearby. Try to shop at a farmer's market whenever possible.

If you don't live in Hawai'i, you're not going to be able to find things like Kahuku corn, Maui Gold pineapples, or Maui onions, but you can make intelligent substitutions. (Please refer to the Glossary & Substitutions at the back of the book.)

For readers who live in Hawai'i, most of the fish and shellfish are available at local supermarkets or fish markets, so I have minimized instructions for cleaning—scaling, gutting, all that. Make good friends with the knowledgeable people behind the counter and listen to their advice.

The Hawaiian fisheries are generally well-regulated as we're trying hard to preserve our ocean resources for future generations. If you're buying local fish and shellfish from a local market or getting it from fishermen friends who obey the regulations, you can be sure that you're being environmentally responsible.

A few recipes call for imported seafood, which can be frozen or has been frozen before shipping and then thawed here. I like to cook the frozen tako (octopus) imported from Japan (Yanagi brand). I also use the frozen surf clams (hokki-gai) from Canada. They come already cleaned, which is convenient.

When buying imported frozen seafood, you have less assurance that the food will be of good quality and from well-managed fisheries. Visit these websites if you want to know more:

Monterey Bay Aquarium: xwww.seafoodwatch.org
Sea Choice: www.seachoice.org
Fishonline: www.fishonline.org

If you live outside of Hawai'i, you should, as much as possible, cook with the fish that's fresh and local where you live. You may want to do your own research. As to what is environmentally responsible and safe to eat, this is a big subject, on which there's a lot of controversy. You might want to consult a few of the major national websites that track seafood safety and sustainability by area.

Many of the Asian ingredients used in the recipes can be found in Asian markets or imported or ethnic food sections in your local markets. Here are the real key ones for making poke.

'Inamona is a traditional Native Hawaiian condiment made with pounded roasted kukui nuts mixed with salt. You won't find it in most supermarkets, but it can be found at many fish markets. If you can't find ready-made 'inamona anywhere, you can substitute mashed, roasted, salted cashews or brazil nuts.

Hawaiian salt is made the traditional way, by evaporating seawater in pans by the seashore. It's more expensive than regular salt, but it adds a unique taste

to the dish. Buy some and try it. If you're living outside Hawai'i, use whatever sea salt or artisanal salt is available and strikes your fancy.

Some recipes call for coconut milk. Fresh coconut milk is usually hard to get, but you can buy it canned or frozen.

A number of recipes call for a dash of Sriracha sauce. This Asian-style hot sauce is made with chilies, garlic, sugar, and vinegar. It comes in a squeeze bottle that makes it very easy to give food a kick that only hot chili peppers can give.

There's also a local Hawai'i alternative to Sriracha: chili-pepper water. This homemade sauce is the essence of convenience and frugality: just chop up some chili peppers, perhaps some garlic, and soak in water. (See the recipe on page 136.)

I also like to use gochujang, or Korean chili paste, also available at most supermarkets. There are a few recipes that call for sambal, or sambal olek, which is a Southeast Asian chili paste. You may have to visit an ethnic market or specialty store to find this.

Furikake is a mixture of dried seaweed, dried fish flakes, chili pepper flakes, salt, and other tasty ingredients. Hawai'i folks eat lots of furikake—sprinkling it on rice, on fish, on all kinds of foods. In the Islands, you can find many blends and brands of furikake at every supermarket. Use your favorite one. You may not find furikake in Mainland supermarkets, but you should be able to buy it at Japanese grocery stores.

Above all else, enjoy. Remember: you are the captain of your kitchen.

Poke 101: Step-by-Step Preparation

The secret to great poke is fresh fish. The ultimate challenge is to catch the fish.

1. Prep the fish for removing the skin by removing back fins, pectoral fins, belly fins, and collar.

2. Remove the innards and prepare to remove the head. Cut a half-inch all the way around the fish, getting ready to separate the fillets.

3. Remove the skin by using a cloth or wet paper towel to wrap your fingers, giving you better grip to grab the skin. Pull the skin straight back on the same level as the fish.

4. As you can see in the photos, we are continuing to remove the skin of the fish.

5. Start to fillet the fish by running your knife all the way to the center bone and prepare for instruction in photo six.

6. Run your knife from the tail all the way to the front of the fish to remove the fillet from the top.

7. Start to quarter the fillets off the bone. Make sure to remove all of the bones.

8. After removing all of the bones, remove the red blood lines.

9. Start to portion the fish into blocks.

10. Make sure there are no bones and no blood. Cut the fish into strips.

11. Cut the strips into cubes.

12. Now you have a bowl of cubed fish just waiting to become the delicacy we call poke.

13. Chop all the ingredients you will be using to make your poke. Add shoyu and seasoning, and mix.

14. Serve your poke cold and fresh with the beverage of your choice. Most times, poke goes great with beer. Enjoy!

Traditional Poke

These old-style Hawaiian poke recipes are ideal if you are making poke for the first time. They highlight the original tastes and flavors of the early poke dishes and are the easiest to make—just some fish, salt, seaweed, maybe some 'inamona. Some have chilies (introduced in the nineteenth century), onions, and tomatoes as well.

Some of the recipes differ only by a single ingredient or type of fish. That's poke's versatility. Just one small change shifts the balance of flavors, resulting in an entirely different taste. With these recipes you can enjoy poke as it was once eaten. The exotic evolution came later, as we shall see in the following chapters.

Before Captain Cook Poke

Serves 4 as appetizer

This simple but delicious poke is just the sort of poke that the people of old would have eaten. It's just fish, salt, seaweed, and kukui nut. Lots of ingredients commonly found in modern poke simply did not exist in pre-contact Hawai'i. They are later imports. However, this poke is proof that the old poke can be tasty too.

If you'd like a little more kick in this dish, you can add the optional chili peppers. Chilies weren't grown in pre-contact Hawai'i. Mary Kawena Pukui thinks that they may have been introduced by Don Marin, in or before 1815. However, early nineteenth-century Hawaiians enthusiastically adopted the new taste and soon chili peppers were being grown, and enjoyed, everywhere in the Islands. After two hundred years, they're traditional too.

- 1 pound sashimi-grade 'ahi, cut into ¾-inch dice
- 1 teaspoon Hawaiian salt
- ¾ cup limu kohu, rinsed and chopped
- 2 Hawaiian chili peppers, trimmed and minced (optional)
- 1½ tablespoons 'inamona

PREPARATION: Mix salt and 'ahi and let stand for 30 minutes in refrigerator. Add the limu, chili peppers, and 'inamona and mix well. Cool the poke, covered, in the refrigerator until you are ready to serve.

Sam deep sea fishing.

Traditional Poke

Straight Hawaiian-Style ʻInamona Poke

Serves 4 as appetizer

This dish brings back memories of picking limu at Lāʻie Bay as a child. This is a classic, and as its name indicates, straightforward recipe. Nothing fancy, just terrific traditional ingredients prepared to perfection.

Oh, I should tell you that Lāʻie Bay is the name on the map. Us locals called it Hukilau Bay. Great place for crabbing and picking limu. If you go drive around Oʻahu and someone says, "That's Hukilau Bay," don't get confused.

1 pound sashimi-grade ʻahi, aku, or other fish, cut into ¾-inch dice
1 small ball limu kohu, rinsed and chopped (makes about ½ cup chopped)
ʻInamona to taste
1 Hawaiian chili pepper, trimeed and minced
Hawaiian salt to taste

PREPARATION: Put all the ingredients into a bowl and mix gently but well. Refrigerate, covered, for 1 hour or more. Serve chilled.

'Ahi Poke Hawaiian-Style #1

Serves 4 to 6 as appetizer

This dish typifies contemporary Hawaiian style. It blends traditional Hawaiian ingredients ('ahi, Hawaiian salt, limu kohu) with Asian touches (shoyu, sesame oil) to create a multi-cultural blend of flavors. I've always maintained that Hawai'i is at the crossroads of the culinary universe; this simple but tasty dish is case in point.

> 1 pound sashimi-grade 'ahi, cut into ¾-inch dice
> ½ cup onion, peeled and chopped
> 2 tablespoons shoyu
> 1 teaspoon sesame oil
> ½ teaspoon granulated sugar
> ½ teaspoon red chili pepper flakes, OR 1 Hawaiian chili pepper, trimmed and minced
> 2 tablespoons green onion, chopped for garnish

PREPARATION: Combine the 'ahi, onion, shoyu, sesame oil, sugar, and the red chili pepper flakes or minced chili pepper. Mix well. Allow flavors to blend for 1 hour before serving. Garnish with the chopped green onion before serving.

Sam and a freshly caught 'ahi.

'Ahi Poke Hawaiian-Style #2

Serves 3 to 4 as appetizer

Another 'ahi poke. Try them all! The differences are subtle, but intriguing.

    1 pound sashimi-grade 'ahi, cut into ¾-inch dice
    ½ cup limu kohu, rinsed and chopped
    ¼ cup Maui onion, peeled and minced
    ¼ cup green onion, chopped
    2 Hawaiian chili peppers, trimmed and minced
    2 tablespoons shoyu
    1 tablespoon sesame oil
    1 teaspoon Hawaiian salt (or add to taste)

PREPARATION: Place all the ingredients into a bowl and mix well. Chill.

Spicy 'Ahi Poke

Serves 4 to 6 as appetizer

This poke is hot! If you like poke with zing, you'll like this. This poke is also tasty if made with fresh salmon. Just use 1½ pounds of salmon in place of the 'ahi.

    1½ pounds sashimi-grade 'ahi, cut into ¾-inch dice
    2 tablespoons green onion, finely chopped
    1 tablespoon onion, peeled and finely chopped
    ½ cup mayonnaise
    3 tablespoons shoyu
    1½ tablespoons chili-pepper oil
    1 teaspoon Sriracha hot sauce

PREPARATION: Cut the 'ahi. Combine all the ingredients in a large bowl. Mix gently until the 'ahi is evenly coated; chill.

Spicy 'Ahi Tomato Poke

Serves 4 as appetizer or 2 as entrée

This recipe is based on Roy T. Kaneko's recipe called 'Ahi Poke Temaki (hand-roll) from my annual poke contest. I add tomatoes, preferably local farm-fresh tomatoes. The heat from the red pepper flakes and the sweetness from the tomato will awaken your taste buds. Serve this chilled. Or as an option you can flash-fry the poke and serve it as a main course.

> 1 pound sashimi-grade 'ahi, cut into ¾-inch dice
> 1 medium-size tomato, trimmed and cut into ¼-inch dice
> ½ cup onion, peeled and chopped
> 2 tablespoons shoyu
> 1 teaspoon sesame oil
> ½ teaspoon granulated sugar
> ½ teaspoon red chili pepper flakes, OR 1 Hawaiian chili pepper, trimmed and minced
> 2 tablespoons green onion, for garnish

PREPARATION: Put the fish, tomato, onion, shoyu, sesame oil, sugar, and pepper flakes or minced pepper in a bowl. Mix gently but well. Allow flavors to blend for 1 hour before serving.

Just before serving, chop the green onion. Sprinkle it over the chilled poke. Serve the poke at once.

Traditional Poke

Spicy Crunchy 'Ahi Poke

Serves 4 as appetizer

This poke contains lots of fresh vegetables, which form a delicious contrast to the 'ahi. The final touch is supplied by the chili peppers and the gochujang sauce, which will make this poke hot.

How hot? Depends on your tastes and your tolerance. It can be "make me sweat a little" hot or "burn da mouth" hot. You can adjust the seasonings to your liking, or, you can keep two scoops rice or some poi handy, to counteract the heat.

> 1 pound sashimi-grade 'ahi, cut into ¾-inch dice
> 1 medium-size tomato, trimmed and cut into ¼-inch dice
> 1 cup ogo, rinsed and chopped
> ½ cup onion, peeled and chopped
> 1 cup cucumber, peeled, seeded, and cut into ¼-inch dice
> ½ cup green onion, finely sliced
> ½ teaspoon Hawaiian chili pepper, trimmed and minced
> 2 tablespoons shoyu
> 1 teaspoon sesame oil
> 1 teaspoon gochujang sauce
> Salt and pepper to taste

PREPARATION: Put all the ingredients into a bowl and mix gently but well. If you're worried that the poke will be too hot for you, add the chilies and gochujang sauce in increments, tasting as you go. Stop when it's hot enough. Finish by adding salt and pepper to taste. Cover and chill before serving.

Aku Poke

Serves 4 as appetizer

Ah, aku. I do a lot of fishing out there on the waters. I see the aku jumping all over the place and I know that there's a big a'u or 'ahi out there trying to get them. It's interesting to see the food chain in the ocean: the aku chase the small shrimps, nehu (anchovies), or squid. Then right above them are the big predators—'ahi and a'u. And right above them are the sharks. Everybody has his place in the food chain.

You can use whatever kind of seaweed looks good when you visit the market: I like to use limu manauea (ogo), līpoa, wāwae'iole, limu kohu, or a combination.

1 pound aku or sashimi-grade 'ahi, cut into ½- or ¾-inch dice
1 cup fresh seaweed, rinsed and chopped
½ cup onion, peeled and chopped
1 Hawaiian chili pepper, trimmed and minced, OR
　　½ teaspoon red chili pepper flakes
2 tablespoons shoyu
1 teaspoon sesame oil

PREPARATION: Combine all the ingredients and mix well. Refrigerate in a covered bowl until ready to serve.

Catching tuna on the Orion.

Dried Aku Poke

Serves 2

Now, this is a favorite of the patrons at my restaurant. However, it took a long time to perfect.

It started when I was trying to find a use for some extra dried aku. After some trial and error, I at last settled on dicing the aku and mixing it with some common poke ingredients (shoyu, sesame oil, etc.). Still, the final product lacked something. Finally I thought of adding some Hawaiian chili peppers; they gave the poke the kick it needed.

Try this at home—I bet you'll fall in love with it too.

> ½ pound dried aku, diced (yields about 2½ cups diced)
> 1 cup ogo, rinsed and chopped
> 1 medium-size Maui onion, peeled and sliced
> 1½ tablespoons shoyu
> 1½ tablespoons sesame oil
> 1½ tablespoons sesame seeds
> 2 Hawaiian chili peppers, trimmed and minced

PREPARATION: Mix all the ingredients and enjoy. It's that easy!

Sam at one of his poke festivals.

My Favorite Easy-Kine Poke

Serves 8 as appetizer, 4 as light entrée

I wanted to make a simple introductory dish for eaters new to the poke experience or for firsttime cooks looking for an easy-to-prepare recipe. There's nothing tricky about this recipe. The ingredients are readily available and easy to prepare. It's also delicious!

> 2 pounds dried aku, cut into ¾-inch dice
> ¼ cup sesame oil
> 1 tablespoon shoyu
> 3 to 4 Hawaiian chili peppers, trimmed and minced (fewer if you
> don't want your poke to be too hot)
> ½ cup ogo, rinsed and chopped
> 1 cup Maui onion, peeled and cut into ¼-inch dice

PREPARATION: Put the dry aku, sesame oil, shoyu, and chili peppers in a large bowl and mix well. Fold in the rest of ingredients and chill, covered.

Smoked A'u Poke

Serves 6 to 8 as appetizer, 3 to 4 as entrée

This variation on my fresh a'u poke is made with smoked a'u. Its simplicity allows the wonderful smoky taste of the a'u to take center stage. A'u is known as marlin on the mainland. It's a big fish, with firm red meat that tastes wonderful when it's smoked.

> 2 pounds smoked a'u, cut into ½-inch dice
> 3 to 4 Hawaiian chili peppers, trimmed and minced (fewer if you
>   don't like spicy poke)
> ¼ cup sesame oil
> 1 tablespoon shoyu
> 1 cup Maui onion, peeled and cut into ¼-inch dice
> ½ cup ogo, rinsed and chopped

PREPARATION: Put the cubed fish, chili pepper, sesame oil, and shoyu in a bowl and mix. Add the onion and ogo and mix again. Chill, covered, until time to serve.

Aʻu Poke

Serves 3 to 4 as appetizer

The aʻu meat featured in this poke is very crisp: it's firm and when it's fresh, has a bit of snap when you bite into it. Aʻu gives a whole new perspective to the traditional poke condiments.

This poke also tastes delicious when it's flash-fried. Just heat a skillet over medium-high heat, fry the poke for just a couple of minutes, and serve on a bed of shredded cabbage.

> 1 pound aʻu, cut into ¾-inch dice
> ¾ cup ogo, rinsed and chopped
> ¼ cup onion, peeled and minced
> ¼ cup green onion, chopped
> 2 to 3 Hawaiian chili peppers, trimmed and minced
> ¼ cup shoyu
> 2 tablespoons roasted sesame seeds
> 1 tablespoon sesame oil
> 1 teaspoon sugar
> Rock salt to taste

PREPARATION: Put all the ingredients into a bowl and mix gently but well. Chill, covered, in the refrigerator for 1 hour or more.

Ono Poke

Serves 3 to 4 as appetizer, 2 as entrée

Ono is a popular fish, but it's rarely used in poke, possibly because it tends to have a dry, firm texture. I've found that the texture gives this poke a wonderfully light flavor. This dish has become a favorite at my restaurant. You'll also find this fish sold as wahoo.

1 pound ono (wahoo), cut into ¾-inch dice
1 cup ogo, rinsed and chopped
¼ cup onion, peeled and minced
¼ cup green onion, minced
2 Hawaiian chili peppers,
   trimmed and minced (add
   more if you like spicy poke)
1 tablespoon 'inamona
2 tablespoons shoyu
1 tablespoon sesame oil
1 teaspoon Hawaiian salt

PREPARATION: Put all the ingredients into a bowl and mix gently but well. Chill, covered, in the refrigerator.

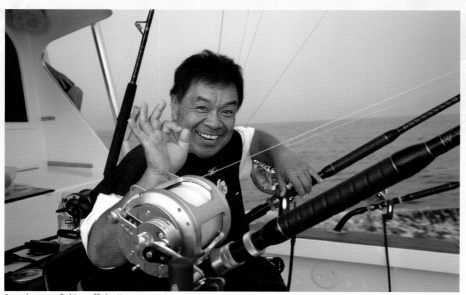

Sam deep sea fishing off the Kona coast.

Korean Tako Poke

Serves 4 to 6 as appetizer

Tako's firm texture and rich taste are complemented by the complex marinade and the crunchy onions. The Korean gochujang paste adds an emphatic hot accent. This is an easy homestyle poke; make it, chill it, sit down with a cold drink and some friends, eat poke, and talk story.

If you're worried that it might be too hot for you, add the paste a little bit at a time and taste after each addition.

> 1½ pounds cooked tako (octopus), cut into ¾-inch dice
> ¼ cup onion, minced
> ¼ cup green onion, chopped
> 2½ tablespoons shoyu
> 1½ tablespoons sesame oil
> 1 tablespoon sesame seed
> 1 tablespoon sugar
> 1½ teaspoons gochujang sauce

PREPARATION: Put all the ingredients into a bowl and mix gently but well. Cover and refrigerate until ready to serve.

Tako Poke

Serves 4 to 6 as appetizer

Tako (he'e in Hawaiian) was a favorite of the people of old. They ate every bit of this delicacy, including the ink. Tako is one of my favorites too. It stars in this poke recipe. It can be a little chewy, but the taste is sublime.

I like to buy the frozen Japanese tako (Yanagi brand), which has already been cleaned. If you started with raw fresh tako, you're going to have to clean it first, or have the fish market clean it. I strongly recommend letting them do it if you aren't an experienced tako cook.

1 pound tako (octopus)

For the relish:
1 ripe medium-size tomato, trimmed and cut into ¼-inch dice
1 cup cucumber, peeled and chopped
½ cup onion, chopped
1 Hawaiian chili pepper, trimmed and minced, OR ½ teaspoon red
   chili pepper flakes
3 tablespoons shoyu
1 teaspoon sesame oil

TO PREPARE THE TAKO: If you've bought frozen tako, thaw it. Tenderize the tako. You can do this by putting it into a bowl and pounding it with a large pestle. You can freeze and then thaw the tako. You can also sprinkle it with tenderizer.

Put some water in a medium-size pot: just enough water to cover the tako. (Some chefs like to use beer or sake for this, but I think water is good enough.) Bring the water to a boil. Lower the tako into the boiling water. Return the water to a rolling boil and cook for another 2 or 3 minutes. Remove the tako from the boiling water and plunge it into a bowl of ice water to stop the cooking. It is very important not to overcook the tako; it gets rubbery when overcooked. When it has cooled, drain it and cut it into very thin slices.

TO PREPARE THE RELISH: Put all the ingredients into a bowl and mix gently but well. Chill, covered, before serving.

Nouveau Poke

Here's the new wave, the cutting-edge poke that my fellow chefs and I have been creating as we explore and experiment, taking this versatile dish to new levels. We are adding peanut butter, lemongrass, crushed macadamia nuts, and other novel ingredients; we are mixing the fish with deep-fried tofu; we are creating elaborate entrées with rice, noodles, and crisp fried tortillas. You'll be surprised, you'll be amazed, and you'll ask for seconds.

Papa's Peanut Butter Poke

Serves 4 to 6 as appetizer

My father created this recipe. I can still remember first tasting it as a child. I'm fortunate that he passed the secret on to me. It's so good, and so special to me, that a part of me would like to keep it secret. But... sharing is the Island way.

I think you'll like the contrast between the crunchy peanut butter, the fiery chili oil, and the smooth taste of the 'ahi. I'm putting this poke first because it shows that way back when, chefs like my dad were starting to experiment. I guess I'm following in his footsteps.

1½ pounds sashimi-grade 'ahi, cut into ¾-inch dice
¼ cup Maui onion, peeled and minced
¼ cup green onion, chopped
2 tablespoons creamy peanut butter
2 tablespoons roasted sesame seeds
1½ tablespoons shoyu
1 tablespoon sesame oil
1 tablespoon chili oil

PREPARATION: Put all the ingredients into a bowl and mix gently but well. Chill, covered.

Sam Choy and his son Sam, Jr. on board the Magic Marlin II.

Sam-Style Poke

Serves 8 as appetizer, 4 as entrée

This is poke my way. The secret is in the sauce.

> 2 pounds sashimi-grade 'ahi, cut into ¾-inch dice
> 1 cup ogo, rinsed and chopped
> 4 teaspoons 'inamona
> 1 tablespoon sesame oil
> 1 teaspoon shoyu
> ⅔ cup Sam's Secret Sauce (see recipe on page 136)

PREPARATION: Combine the 'ahi with the ogo, 'inamona, sesame oil, and shoyu. Mix thoroughly. Add Sam's Secret Sauce and mix again. Refrigerate, covered, for 30 to 60 minutes before serving. This allows the flavors to marry.

Asian-Style Poke

Serves 6 to 8 as appetizer, 3 to 4 as entrée

What makes this poke Asian? Furikake, a salty mixture of dried fish, seaweed, sesame seed, and other tasty-kine stuff that so many Island folks like to sprinkle on their rice, their fish, and many other foods. It's just the right garnish for an innovative 'ahi poke.

> 2 pounds sashimi-grade 'ahi, cut into ¾-inch dice
> 1 cup ogo, rinsed and chopped
> ⅓ cup onion, peeled and finely chopped
> 1 tablespoon green onion, chopped
> ¼ cup furikake
> ½ teaspoon red chili pepper flakes
> 2 tablespoons sesame oil
> 1 tablespoon balsamic vinegar
> 1 tablespoon granulated sugar
> 1 tablespoon shoyu

PREPARATION: Put all the ingredients into a bowl and mix well. Refrigerate, covered, until ready to serve.

'Ahi King Poke

Serves 4 as appetizer

This is another favorite of mine. As I was concocting the recipe, I felt that the taste of the dish was somewhat familiar and that the flavors weren't sufficiently highlighted. Then I hit upon the idea of adding my Original Asian Creamy Dressing, which gives the dish some texture as well as a richer taste. The results speak for themselves.

> 1 pound sashimi-grade 'ahi, cut into ¾-inch dice
> 1½ cups onion, peeled and finely sliced (about 1 medium-size onion)
> ¼ cup green onion, chopped
> 1 teaspoon rock salt
> White pepper to taste
> 2 tablespoons shoyu
> 1 teaspoon Tabasco® sauce
> 3 tablespoons Sam Choy's Original Asian Creamy Dressing (see recipe on page 143)

PREPARATION: Put the fish, onion, green onion, salt, pepper, shoyu and Tabasco® sauce in a large bowl and mix well. Add the Dressing and mix again.

Slicing freshly caught 'ahi still on the fishing boat.

Nouveau Poke

Oven-Roasted Garlic 'Ahi Poke

Serves 4 as appetizer

Here's another dish that adds an unexpected ingredient to 'ahi poke. The ingredient: roasted garlic. When garlic is drizzled with olive oil and baked, it becomes sweet, mellow, and nutty. Fold it into poke and take a nibble. Your taste buds will fall in love.

    1 whole garlic bulb
    1 tablespoon olive oil
    1 pound sashimi-grade 'ahi, cut into ¾-inch dice
    ½ cup ogo, rinsed and chopped
    ¾ cup Maui onion, peeled and minced (about ½ medium onion)
    1 or 2 Hawaiian chili peppers, trimmed and minced
    1 tablespoon shoyu
    ½ tablespoon sesame oil
    ½ teaspoon Hawaiian salt
    White pepper to taste

PREPARATION: Pull off the outer layers of the garlic bulb, leaving only the peel on the individual cloves. Cut off the pointed end of the garlic bulb, exposing the ends of the cloves. Put the bulb in a garlic roaster or just place it on a square of aluminum foil. Drizzle the olive oil over the exposed ends of the garlic cloves. Close the roaster or wrap up the garlic in the foil. Roast for 35 to 40 minutes at 350°F. Let the bulb cool and then squeeze or pry the roasted garlic out of the peel. Put the soft roasted garlic in a small bowl and mix until you have a soft paste.

Put the 'ahi, ogo, onion, chili pepper, shoyu, sesame oil, salt, and pepper in a large bowl and mix gently but well. Fold the roasted garlic into the poke.

'Ahi Poke with Mac Nuts

Serves 4 as appetizer

Even though many people think of the Islands when they think of macadamia nuts, these nuts are not native to Hawai'i. The crop was introduced in the nineteenth century and has since become a major export. The tasty nuts have also been welcomed into Island cuisine, where they feature in many recipes.

I decided to create a poke that blended ancient Hawaiian ingredients with a more modern flavor. After some experimentation, I created this nouveau poke. Macadamia nuts and the crisp ogo seaweed give this poke a wonderful, nutty crunch.

1 pound sashimi-grade 'ahi, cut into ½-inch dice
4.5 ounces (1 can) Hawai'i Island unsalted macadamia nuts,
  chopped
½ cup ogo, rinsed and chopped
⅓ cup green onion, chopped
3 Hawaiian chili peppers, trimmed and
  minced
2 tablespoons shoyu
1 tablespoon Hawaiian salt
1 tablespoon sesame oil

Sam fishing aboard the Magic Marlin II.

PREPARATION: Put all the ingredients into a large bowl and mix gently but well. Chill, covered.

'Ahi Poke Salad

Serves 4 as appetizer

Poke continues to evolve in new and exciting ways. Case in point: this salad combines three distinct influences. There is Hawaiian influence in the poke, Japanese influence in the shoyu and somen, and Latin American influence in the simple, versatile tortilla, which gives the dish some crunch and texture. The result is a wonderful blend of cultures and a study in contrasts.

For the poke:
1 pound sashimi-grade 'ahi, cut into ¾-inch dice
¼ cup onion, peeled and chopped
¼ cup green onion, chopped
¼ cup ogo, rinsed and chopped
½ cup cup shoyu
¼ cup sesame oil

For the poke garnishes:
2 cups cooked somen (thin Japanese wheat noodles)
3 cups mixed fresh salad greens
½ cup canola oil or as needed for frying
8 (10-inch) wheat flour tortillas

PREPARATION: Mix the 'ahi, onion, green onion, ogo, shoyu, and sesame oil in a bowl. Cover and chill.

Cook the somen according to the package directions. Rinse and drain. Wash the salad greens and tear them into bite-size pieces.

Heat the oil in a frying pan over medium-high heat. Fry the tortillas, one at a time, until they are golden-brown. Blot them with paper towels to remove any excess oil.

Set out 4 serving plates. On each plate, put 1 tortilla. Put a handful of greens on each tortilla. Add another tortilla to each stack. Put ¼ of the somen on each stack, then ¼ of the poke. Serve immediately; if you wait, the tortillas will get soggy.

Pesto Poke

Serves 6 to 8 as appetizer, 3 to 4 as entrée

Traditional Italian pesto is made from young basil leaves, pine nuts, garlic, and olive oil. I wanted to make a pesto that used familiar Island flavors, so I substituted green onion and cilantro for the basil, macadamia nuts for the pine nuts, and ginger for the garlic. The pesto is made with a neutral-flavored vegetable oil rather than a more assertive olive oil.

As with so many of my recipes, I start with a traditional concept (the Italian pesto), substitute local ingredients and flavors, and end up with something that is both cross-cultural and utterly delicious. Naturally, my Island pesto tastes divine on raw fish.

2½ pounds sashimi-grade ʻahi, cut into ¾-inch dice
2 tablespoons coarse salt
Lettuce for wraps (optional)

For the Island Pesto:
½ cup green onion, chopped
½ cup cilantro, chopped
¼ cup ginger, peeled and choppped
2 Hawaiian chili peppers, trimmed and choppped
½ cup macadamia nuts, finely chopped
¾ cup vegetable oil

PREPARATION: Put the ʻahi in a medium-size bowl or container and mix with the coarse salt gently, with your hand.

Put the green onion, cilantro, ginger, chili peppers, macadamia nuts, and vegetable oil into the bowl of a food processor and process into pesto.

When the salt mixed with the ʻahi has completely dissolved, add the pesto. Mix gently but well. Cover the poke and chill for 1 to 2 hours.

If you want to get fancy, wash and trim some lettuce leaves. Wrap a nice bite of poke in a leaf; repeat until you've wrapped up all of the poke.

Thai 'Ahi Poke with Lemongrass

Serves 3 to 4 as appetizer

Lemongrass is native to Malaysia, but is now grown and eaten all across Southeast Asia. It is also used in Indian and Chinese cooking—and increasingly, in Western cuisine as well. Its light lemon taste (with a bit of a bite) adds interest to so many dishes. Here, it adds pizzazz to an 'ahi poke. Mint and lime add their fresh flavors as well. If you had to pick one word to describe this dish, that word would be "refreshing."

> 1 pound sashimi-grade 'ahi, cut into ½-inch dice
> ¼ cup red onion, peeled and sliced thin
> ¼ cup green onion, chopped
> 2 Hawaiian chili peppers, trimmed, seeded, and minced
> 2 habanero peppers, trimmed, seeded, and minced
> 5 to 6 fresh mint leaves, slivered
> 2 tablespoons lime juice (about 1 lime)
> 1 teaspoon lemongrass (approximately ½ stalk,
>   the lower half), finely minced
> ½ teaspoon Hawaiian salt
> White pepper to taste

For the garnish:
¼ cup chopped cilantro

PREPARATION: Peel the tough outer leaves from the lemongrass. Trim off the bulb at the end of the stalk. Cut the stalk into slices as thin as you can manage. You can use them as is, or, if you'd like them to be a little softer, put them in a mortar and pound them with a pestle.

Put the cubed fish, red onion, green onion, peppers, mint, lime, lemongrass, salt, and pepper in a bowl and mix well. Put in your serving dish, cover, and chill for at least 1 hour.

While the poke is chilling, you can chop the cilantro. Sprinkle the cilantro over the poke and serve chilled.

This poke is also great served in a summer-roll wrapper and garnished with other vegetables.

Nouveau Poke

Poke 'Ahi Bowl

Serves 1 as entrée

Need a quick meal? Got some poke in the fridge? Cook up some rice and put the poke over the hot rice. The juices from the poke will flavor the rice; the heat from the rice will cook the outside of the poke a little. A drizzle of one of my aioli sauces is the final touch.

I've included a recipe for a simple 'ahi poke that will taste great with or without rice. However, you can use just about any poke in this book and still end up with a tasty treat.

For the poke:
½ pound sashimi-grade 'ahi, cut into ¾-inch dice (about 1 cup cubed)
¼ cup onion, peeled and minced
¼ cup green onion, chopped
½ teaspoon ginger, peeled and minced
1 Hawaiian chili pepper, trimmed and minced
1 tablespoon shoyu
½ tablespoon sesame oil

For serving:
1½ cups plain or Sushi Rice (see recipe on page 101)
A drizzle of Honey Wasabi Aioli, OR Spicy Honey Aioli (see recipes on pages 138, 139)

TO MAKE THE POKE: Put the fish, onion, green onion, ginger, chili pepper, shoyu, and sesame oil in a medium-size bowl and mix well. Cover and chill.

Put the sushi rice into bowls or on a platter. Top with poke. Drizzle Honey Wasabi Aioli or Spicy Honey Aioli over the top.

Poke Pie

Serves 4 to 6 as appetizer

This is a very modern poke presentation. Chefs say that "we eat with our eyes first." According to some recent scientific studies, that's absolutely true: we eat more and absorb more nutrients from our food when it's presented in an appealing way. Here's a poke pie that will ravish your eyes and then your palate.

- 1¼ pounds sashimi-grade 'ahi, minced (makes about 2½ cups minced)
- ½ cup lump crabmeat, shredded, OR ½ cup chopped kamaboko (Japanese fishcake)
- 1 + 1 tablespoons tobiko (flying fish roe), separated
- 1 medium onion, peeled and chopped
- ½ + ¼ cup green onion, sliced, separated
- ¾ cup mayonnaise
- 2½ tablespoons shoyu
- 2 tablespoons sesame oil
- 1 tablespoon Sriracha hot sauce
- 2 cups wasabi furikake
- 4 cups cooked rice
- 2 tablespoons sesame seeds
- 1.8 ounces (1 package) Korean seasoned nori (optional)

PREPARATION: Combine the 'ahi, crabmeat or kamaboko (Japanese fishcake), 1 tablespoon of the tobiko, onion, ½ cup of the green onion, mayonnaise, shoyu, sesame oil, and Sriracha hot sauce in a medium-size bowl. Cover and refrigerate. The poke should rest and marinate for at least 30 minutes.

The 1 tablespoon of tobiko and ¼ cup of green onion that you didn't put into the poke should be set aside; you will use them to garnish the finished dish.

TO ASSEMBLE: Sprinkle ½ cup of the wasabi furikake over the bottom of a 9-inch diameter pie pan; add the cooked rice and spread evenly. Spread a layer of poke evenly over the rice. Sprinkle the top with remaining tobiko, remaining green onion, and sesame seeds. Chill.

For individual servings, set out 4 to 6 small plates and put a piece of Korean seasoned nori on each. Spoon some of the poke pie onto each plate. To serve family-style, simply set the pie on the table and let the family dig in.

Family-Style Cold Soba Noodles with Aku Poke

Serves 4 as entrée

I often bring this simple, hearty dish to parties and get-togethers. The flavors in this recipe are very distinct: the mellow taste of the sesame oil and the salty shoyu are complemented by the sweetness of the sugar and the acidity of the lime. The result is a blend of flavors that will leave everyone at the table wanting more. Make plenty! To give this dish a bit more kick, add bits of cooked salmon.

7 ounces dried soba noodles
4 cups shredded lettuce (your favorite kind)

For the poke:
2 pounds aku, cubed
2 average-size tomatoes, trimmed and chopped
1½ cups ogo, rinsed and chopped
¼ cup green onion, minced
1 Hawaiian chili pepper, trimmed and minced
4 tablespoons shoyu
1½ tablespoons sesame oil

For the dressing:
¾ cup sesame oil
2½ tablespoons rice vinegar
2½ tablespoons shoyu
1 tablespoon raw sugar
Zest and juice of one average-size lime
1 teaspoon garlic, peeled and minced
½ cup carrots, peeled and julienned
½ cup cilantro, chopped
2 tablespoons salted macadamia nuts, chopped

TO MAKE THE POKE: In a large bowl, mix the fish, tomato, ogo, green onion, chili pepper, shoyu, and sesame oil. Cover and chill until ready to serve.

Continued on page 44

TO PREPARE THE NOODLES: Heat water in a medium pot and cook soba noodles according to package directions. Drain and rinse in cold running water to stop the cooking. Drain again and set aside.

TO PREPARE THE NOODLE DRESSING: Put the sesame oil, rice vinegar, shoyu, sugar, lime juice and zest, and garlic in a large bowl and mix well. Add the carrots, cilantro, and macadamia nuts to the dressing and mix again.

Wash, dry, and shred the lettuce. Spread it on a serving platter and heap the noodles on top. Pour the dressing over the noodles. Cover the platter and let the noodles marinate and chill for at least 1 hour. Remove the platter of chilled noodles from the refrigerator and top with the poke.

Tako with Honey Miso Vinaigrette

Serves 4 to 6 as appetizer or light meal

I think of this as a sushi bar recipe—it reminds me of dishes I've eaten on my travels throughout Japan. It's a simple dish but a good and popular one. The tako (octopus) is very firm and goes well with the sweet Maui onions. Drizzle Honey Miso Vinaigrette over the top and the dressing will take this salad from good to great.

You can buy cooked tako at the supermarket or fish market. You can also use frozen tako. I often buy the frozen tako imported from Japan under the Yanagi label.

> 2–3 pounds cooked tako (octopus), cut into ¼-inch dice
> ½ cup Maui onion, peeled and sliced
> ½ cup green onion, chopped
> 2 medium-size tomatoes, trimmed and cut into ¼-inch dice
> 1½ cups Honey Miso Vinaigrette (see recipe on page 141)
> 3 cups mesclun, mixed greens, or lettuce of your choice; washed, dried, and torn into bite-size pieces

PREPARATION: Put the tako, onion, green onion, and tomatoes in a large bowl and mix gently but well. Chill, covered, before serving.

Serve the poke on a bed of lettuce, with Honey Miso Vinaigarette on the side as a dip. Oh so goood!

Wasabi Ono Poke with Tobiko

Serves 4 as appetizer, 2 as entrée

This is one of my "new wave" or nouveau poke dishes. It takes a few traditional ingredients and combines them with new flavors and textures. In this dish, I use tobiko (flying fish roe) and wasabi. Tobiko, like caviar, has a beguiling crunch; the wasabi gives spice and heat.

1 pound ono (wahoo), cut into ¾-inch dice
½ cup red onion, peeled and thinly sliced
¼ cup green onion, chopped
¼ cup ogo, rinsed and chopped
2 tablespoons tobiko (flying fish roe)
1 tablespoon kuro goma (black sesame
   seeds)

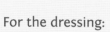

For the dressing:
1 tablespoon lemongrass (may take several stalks),
   minced
1 tablespoon ginger, peeled and minced
1 teaspoon garlic, peeled and mashed
2 tablespoons lime juice (about 1 lime)
½ cup olive oil
1 tablespoon sesame oil
1½ ounces wasabi (Japanese horseradish paste)
Salt to taste

PREPARATION: Put the ono, red onion, green onion, ogo, tobiko, and sesame seeds in a bowl and mix well.

If you've just picked the lemongrass from your garden, cut off the leaves at the top, leaving only the stalks. Lemongrass sold in supermarkets is already trimmed. Peel the tough outer leaves from the lemongrass. Trim off the bulb at the end of the stalks. Cut the stalk into slices as thin as you can manage.

Put the ginger, garlic, lemongrass, and lime juice into the bowl of a food processor or blender. With the processor running, slowly pour the olive oil into the dressing. Process until the mixture emulsifies. Add the sesame oil and wasabi, and salt to taste.

Continued on page 47

Add dressing to the ono-tobiko mixture while gently folding. Stop adding dressing when the fish is coated but not wet. You may not need all the dressing. Chill, covered, until time to serve. Serve garnished with a few extra sprigs of ogo.

Spicy 'Ahi and Crab Poke

Serves 4 to 6 as appetizer or light meal

This poke features an unusual mixture of two kinds of seafood ('ahi and crab), the rich taste of mayonnaise, and a hot tingle from Sriracha sauce (Vietnamese hot sauce) and shichimi togarashi (Japanese chili spice). It's the latest hit at my restaurant. Patrons like it on rolls, as a slider. You can also put it in sandwiches or rice balls. If you don't have any fresh crabmeat on hand, you can buy it in cans at most supermarkets.

1½ pounds sashimi-grade 'ahi, minced (should make about 3 cups minced 'ahi)

¼ pound lump crab meat (about 1 cup), shredded

½ cup onion, peeled and minced

½ cup green onion, chopped

3 tablespoons tobiko (flying fish roe)

1½ cups mayonnaise

¼ cup shoyu

2 tablespoons Sriracha hot sauce

½ teaspoon shichimi togarashi (Japanese seven-spice powder)

1 tablespoon sesame oil

PREPARATION: Put all the ingredients into a bowl and mix gently but well.

This poke is delicious served straight out of the bowl. If you're feeling more ambitious, you can roll it up in rice balls, to make musubi, or even turn it into a makizushi roll. You can also serve it with fresh taro rolls and make little poke sliders.

Tofu Poke with Ogo

Serves 3 to 4 as appetizer, 2 as entrée

I serve this poke in my restaurant as a vegetarian alternative to my meat and fish dishes. The deep-fried tofu makes a highly satisfactory replacement for the usual raw fish. The secret here is good deep-frying technique. Keep the oil at the right temperature and the tofu won't be oily or soggy.

> 3 average-size beefsteak tomatoes, trimmed and diced
> 1 average-size Maui onion, peeled and diced
> ½ cup ogo, rinsed and chopped
> ¼ cup green onion, chopped
> 3 tablespoons shoyu
> 2 tablespoons sesame oil
> 2 tablespoons sugar
> 1 tablespoon kuro goma (black sesame seeds)
> 1 teaspoon red chili pepper flakes
> Hawaiian salt to taste
> 1 pound firm tofu, drained and cut into ¾-inch dice
> Cornstarch for dusting
> Peanut oil for deep-frying

PREPARATION: Put the tomatoes, onion, ogo, green onion, shoyu, sesame oil, sugar, sesame seeds, chili flakes, and salt in a bowl and lomi (massage) the ingredients together.

Dust all sides of the tofu cubes with cornstarch. Heat the oil in a deep-fryer or a heavy pot to 350°F. Deep-fry the tofu cubes until golden-brown. Remove from the oil and drain on paper towels.

Add the crisp tofu cubes to the salad and toss to combine. Serve immediately.

Mauka Avocado Poke

Serves 3 to 4 as appetizer, 2 as entrée

The key to this recipe is finding thick creamy, buttery avocados. Accept no substitutes. Be sure to cut the avocados into large chunks. You want big bites of pure avocado flavor; you don't want the avocado to fade into the background. This is a simple dish, but it is very, very good.

2 medium-size avocados, halved, seeded, peeled, and cut into
   1-inch dice
1 cup diced Waimea tomato, cut into ¼-inch dice
½ cup ogo, rinsed and chopped
½ cup Maui onion, peeled and cut into ¼-inch dice
¼ cup green onion, chopped
3 Hawaiian chili peppers, trimmed and minced
1 tablespoon 'inamona
1 tablespoon roasted sesame seeds
2 tablespoons sesame oil
2 tablespoons shoyu

PREPARATION: Put all the ingredients into a glass or ceramic bowl and mix gently but well. Cool, covered, in the refrigerator. Great plain, or with chips or crackers.

Calabash Cousins

Poke isn't the only kind of raw seafood that we eat. All over the world, raw fish and shellfish are consumed in various forms. These recipes are poke adaptations, from the traditional Hawaiian lomilomi to the Polynesian (or South American) ceviches to the Japanese tatakis to the European tartares and carpaccios. Cooking has really gone global, with cuisines from around the world interacting and influencing each other. When it comes to eating, the world is one big harmonious family.

LOMILOMI

Conservation was an essential part of the old culture. These traditional dishes originate in the early Hawaiians' desire not to waste anything that came from the earth or the sea. They present innovative ways to use fish that would otherwise be too bony to eat raw. The fish isn't cut up (poke'd), but massaged (lomied) to find and remove the bones.

Da Big Lomilomi Poke
Serves 4 to 6 as entrée

When dried salted salmon from the U.S. Pacific Northwest was introduced to Hawai'i in the nineteenth century, Hawaiian cooks figured out how to soak it (removing some of the salt) and lomi it (removing the bones). The result was the beloved lomilomi salmon, now a local favorite.

I'm known for stretching boundaries and definitions when it comes to food, but in this case, I've taken a traditional approach. This is classic lomilomi salmon, tweaked and refined until it's the best it can be. (But if you're looking to add some kick, try the optional limu kohu and chilies.) You'll need to start work on this dish one day before you plan to serve it.

> 1 pound fresh salmon, cut into ¾-inch dice
> 1 cup Hawaiian salt
> 1 pound aku, cut into ¾-inch dice (about 2 cups)
> ½ cup 'ōpae (dried shrimp)
> 1½ cups onion, peeled and diced (about 1 medium onion)
> 1 cup green onion, chopped
> 6 to 8 tomatoes, trimmed and cut into ¼-inch dice
> Limu kohu to taste (optional)
> Hawaiian chili peppers, trimmed and minced, to taste (optional)

PREPARATION: Mix the salmon with Hawaiian salt in a sealed plastic bag. Seal the bag and leave it overnight in the refrigerator. The next day, rinse the salmon under cold running water. Check for saltiness. Rinse again if the salmon is too salty.

Put all the ingredients into a large bowl and mix gently but well. Chill, covered, in the refrigerator until ready to serve. This poke is great with poi!

Calabash Cousins

Lomilomi Salmon with a Twist

Serves 4 to 6 as appetizer

If you'd like to try a variation on the classic lomilomi salmon, try this. The twist in the title is the addition of deep-fried dried shrimp. These tasty little 'ōpae are sweet and crunchy. They are a delicious contrast to the softer texture of the fish and tomatoes. The onions and ogo also add crunch.

Note that you'll need to start the dish the day before you plan to serve it.

> 1 pound salted salmon
> 3 cups onion, peeled and cut into ¼-inch dice (about 2 onions)
> ½ cup green onion, chopped
> 2 cups ogo, rinsed and chopped
> 3 ripe medium-size tomatoes, trimmed and cut into ¼-inch dice
> 1 cup dried shrimp
> Vegetable oil for deep-frying (safflower, cottonseed, or corn oil are
>   good)

PREPARATION: Put the salted salmon in a bowl, add fresh water to cover, cover the bowl, and chill overnight in the refrigerator. The next day, drain the salmon and rinse well. Discard salmon skin and bones. Cut salmon into small dice (about ½ inch).

Just before assembling the salad, deep-fry the dried shrimp. Heat oil to 350 to 365°F in a deep-fryer or heavy pot. Put the shrimp in a deep-frying basket, if you have one. Fry shrimp just a few moments or until they are crunchy; remove from oil and drain on a paper towel to remove any extra oil.

Put the salmon, onion, green onion, ogo, and tomatoes in a serving bowl. Add the fried shrimp and mix well. Chill until time to serve.

CEVICHE

Ceviche is raw fish that has been "cooked" by vinegar or citrus juice. Acidic liquids coagulate the proteins in the fish so that the flesh becomes firm and opaque. Ceviche may have been invented in Latin America after the arrival of the Spaniards, and then spread throughout the Pacific by their traveling ships as well as those of other countries. In many of the Polynesian islands, ceviche is marinated with both coconut milk and lime juice and is considered a traditional food.

Tropical 'Ahi Poke

Serves 4 as appetizer

The featured ingredient in this 'ahi ceviche is ... mango! Mango adds an unexpected sweetness, while the bell peppers and cilantro serve as a crisp contrast to the softer fish. The smooth, rich flavor of the coconut milk balances the acid zing of the lemon. I'm very proud of this nouveau poke.

1 pound sashimi-grade 'ahi, cut into ½-inch dice
1 cup fresh mango, peeled, seeded, and cut into ½-inch dice
¼ cup red bell pepper, trimmed, seeded, and cut into ¼-inch dice
¼ cup yellow bell pepper, trimmed, seeded, and cut into ¼-inch dice
2 Hawaiian chili peppers, trimmed and minced
½ cup coconut milk
2 tablespoons lemon juice (about 1 lemon)
2 teaspoons sesame oil
3 tablespoons shoyu
Salt to taste
¼ cup chopped fresh cilantro, as garnish

PREPARATION: Put all the ingredients except the cilantro into a medium-size bowl and mix gently but well. Cover and refrigerate for at least 1 hour before serving. Garnish with the chopped cilantro and serve immediately.

Simply 'Ahi Ceviche

Serves 4 to 6

Many Polynesian ceviche recipes call for long marination times. This ceviche is served immediately after it is assembled. The fish is only partially "cooked" by the lime juice. The outside is "cooked," the inside is still raw. This contrast of flavors and textures is reminiscent of seared sashimi. Try this instant ceviche for a change.

> 1 pound sashimi-grade 'ahi, cut into ¾-inch dice
> 2 medium-size cucumbers, peeled, seeded, and cut into ¼-inch dice
> 2 medium-size round onions, peeled and cut into ¼-inch dice
> 2 medium-size fresh tomatoes, trimmed and cut into ¼-inch dice
> ½ cup green onion, chopped
> 2 + 2 tablespoons (¼ cup total) fresh cilantro, chopped and
>   separated
> Pinch of red chili pepper flakes, or to taste
> ¼ cup lime juice (about 2 limes)
> 2 cups coconut milk
> Salt and pepper to taste

> For the garnish:
> 2 fresh limes, sliced or cut into wedges (with the lime for lime juice,
>   you will need 4 or more limes total)

PREPARATION: Put the 'ahi, cucumber, onion, tomato, green onion, and 2 tablespoons of the cilantro into a bowl. (Reserve 2 tablespoons of cilantro for garnish.) Add the chili flakes. Pour the lime juice into the bowl. Gently stir all of the ingredients together. Add the coconut milk and mix again. Adjust the seasoning with salt and pepper.

Put the fish on individual serving plates or on a platter. Garnish with cilantro and lime slices.

Spicy 'Ahi Ceviche

Serves 4 as appetizer

Here's a ceviche made with lime juice, coconut milk, and olive oil. It combines the Polynesian and South American versions of ceviche. Onion, ginger, and chili peppers add a bit of a kick. For extra coconut flavor, you can add the optional grated coconut. Don't use supermarket dried and sweetened coconut for this; don't use the large mature coconuts sold in many supermarkets. You need a young coconut, past the spoonmeat stage (when the flesh is so soft you can eat it with a spoon) but not yet hard and dry. You can sometimes buy these young coconuts at Asian markets. Just remove the husk (if it's not already removed), crack the coconut open with a hammer, remove the meat from the shell, and grate it.

1 pound sashimi-grade 'ahi, cut into ¾-inch dice
1 tablespoon Hawaiian salt
2 tablespoons olive oil
4 tablespoons lime juice (about 2 limes)
1 cup cucumber, peeled, seeded, and cut into ¼-inch dice
½ cup Maui onion, peeled and finely chopped
2 medium tomatoes, trimmed and diced
3 Hawaiian chili peppers, trimmed and minced
½ tablespoon fresh ginger, peeled and grated
2 cups coconut milk

PREPARATION: Place the 'ahi in a glass or ceramic (non-metalic) bowl. Add the Hawaiian salt, olive oil, and lime juice. Mix so that the marinade coats all the 'ahi pieces. Cover the bowl and refrigerate for 30 minutes.

Check the marinated 'ahi. If the 'ahi is dry, add a little more lime juice. Fold the diced cucumber and finely chopped onion into the 'ahi. Add the tomato, chili peppers, ginger, and coconut milk. Stir to mix. Refrigerate, covered, for at least 1 hour so that the flavors can marry. Enjoy!

Poisson Cru

Serves 4 to 6 as appetizer, 2 to 3 as entrée

Poisson cru is just French for "raw fish." In Tahiti, it's what they call ceviche. This ceviche is made with lots of crisp, fresh veggies and marinated for only a few minutes. You could call it a fish salad. It's a refreshing, cool entrée, perfect for a hot day.

1½ pounds sashimi-grade 'ahi, cut into ½-inch dice
½ cup lime juice (about 2 limes)
1½ cups onion, peeled and cut into ¼-inch dice (about 1 medium onion)
¾ cup bell pepper, trimmed, seeded, and cut into ¼-inch dice (about ½ of a bell pepper)
1 medium tomato, trimmed and cut into ¼-inch dice
1 cup cucumber, peeled, seeded, and diced (about ½ of a cucumber)
1 cup coconut milk
Salt to taste
Green onion, chopped for garnish

PREPARATION: Put the cubed fish into a bowl and mix it with the lime juice. Marinate the fish for 5 minutes, then spoon out half the juice. Add the onion, bell pepper, tomato, cucumber, and coconut milk to the bowl. Add salt to taste. Garnish with chopped green onion and serve.

Mediterranean ʻAhi Poke

Serves 4 as appetizer, 2 as entrée

I typically use sesame oil in my poke recipes. Sesame oil lends a nutty, Asian flavor to any dish. Here, I experimented with using olive oil. It was a revelation. The olive oil is lighter. It lets the other ingredients take the spotlight. Here, it's the bell peppers, tomato, red onion, and Kalamata olives that call for attention.

1 pound sashimi-grade ʻahi, cut into ¾-inch dice (makes about 2 cups diced)
½ cup red bell pepper, trimmed, seeded, and minced
½ cup yellow bell pepper, trimmed, seeded, and minced
¼ cup tomato, trimmed and cut into ¼-inch dice
¼ cup red onion, peeled and minced
12 Kalamata olives, chopped
3 whole habanero peppers, trimmed and minced
3 tablespoons capers
1½ teaspoons salt
4 tablespoons lime juice (about 2 medium limes)
½ cup olive oil

PREPARATION: Put all the ingredients into a glass or ceramic (non-metalic) bowl and mix well. Let stand, covered, in the refrigerator for 30 minutes.

Pitcairn Poke

Serves 4 as appetizer

I created this dish to commemorate my trip to Pitcairn Island. Ono is plentiful there. While I was visiting, I saw schools of ono as large as football fields. Whenever I cook with this fish, I think of my time at Pitcairn.

1 pound ono, cut into ½-inch dice (about 2 cups diced)
1½ cup onion, cut into ¼-inch dice (about 1 medium onion)
¾ cup green onion, chopped
1½ teaspoons salt
1 cup freshly squeezed orange juice (about 2 medium oranges)
1 cup freshly squeezed lemon juice (about 4 average lemons)
½ cup cucumber, peeled, seeded, and cut into ¼-inch dice
¾ cup coconut milk

Residents of Pitcairn Island in 2007.

PREPARATION: Put the fish, chopped onions, green onions, and salt in a bowl and mix well. Add the orange and lemon juices. Cover the bowl and let it stand in the refrigerator for 6 to 8 hours.

If you're using frozen coconut milk, put it out to thaw while the fish is marinating.

Remove the marinated fish from the refrigerator and drain off any excess liquid. Add the diced cucumbers and coconut milk and mix well. Serve immediately.

TARTARE & CARPACCIO

The European raw food tradition gets credit for these recipes. Both tartare and carpaccio were originally made with raw beef, but European chefs have since started making tartares and carpaccios with fish. These are new tastes—great tastes that will surely delight the palate.

Ono Carpaccio with Hot Ginger-Pepper Oil

Serves 4

Classic sashimi is served with just a dash of nikiri (a mixture of shoyu and sake). That's the reason I call this dish a carpaccio: no nikiri. Instead, the raw fish is drizzled with oil, like European carpaccio dishes. The spicy oil gives the dish a delicious kick, while the shredded vegetables, like the shredded daikon served with classic sashimi, are a delicious, crunchy contrast.

> 1 pound ono (wahoo) fillet, cut into ¼-inch thick strips, 2½ inches long and 1¾ inches wide
> 4 tablespoons Hot Ginger-Pepper Oil (see recipe on page 137)

> For the garnish:
> 1½ cups raw vegetables (cabbage, carrot, jicama, or beet)

PREPARATION: If you are using a root vegetable, wash and peel it before shredding or grating. If you are using cabbage, wash, remove any wilted outer leaves, core, cut into quarters, and shred.

PRESENTATION: Spread the shredded vegetables evenly over a small platter. Arrange the raw ono slices over the vegetables. Drizzle the Hot Ginger-Pepper Oil over the fish.

'Ahi Tartare with Ginger

Serves 4 to 6 as appetizer

I find that many people who have reservations about eating poke simply can't get past the idea that it's raw chopped fish. Funny thing—they'll eat raw fish if I call it tartare. They know that steak tartare is a classy European dish, so they're willing to try fish tartare. Once they try it, they usually like it. After that, names don't matter.

1½ pounds sashimi-grade 'ahi, minced
½ cup green onion, minced
½ tablespoon fresh ginger, peeled and minced
2 tablespoons sesame oil
2 tablespoons mirin
1 tablespoon rice vinegar
Salt and pepper to taste

Garnish:
Organic field greens
Edible flowers (sold in supermarket produce sections)
Kuro goma (black sesame seeds)

PREPARATION: Put the 'ahi, green onion, ginger, sesame oil, mirin, and vinegar in a medium-size glass or wooden bowl. Mix well. Season with salt and pepper to taste. Cover and refrigerate until it is time to serve.

I like to serve this poke on a platter covered with organic field greens. I dot the greens with mounds of poke and sprinkle the top of the poke with black sesame seeds. Edible flowers make a pretty edging around the rim of the platter. Of course, this poke would still be 'ono served plain, with chips and beer on the side.

'Ahi Carpaccio Tahitian Style

Serves 6 as appetizer, 3 or 4 as entrée

I learned how to make this dish from my old friend and classmate, Timmi Blanchard, who now runs a restaurant, Snack Bébé, in Tahiti.

European carpaccios are usually thin slices of raw beef or veal, drizzled with oil. Here, I use our wonderful local 'ahi. Capers and Kalamata olives give a European touch, while a last-minute garnish of fresh lime juice adds tanginess. Use Tahitian limes if you can get them. Otherwise, use Calamansis or another variety of thin-skinned lime.

2 pounds sashimi-grade 'ahi, sliced very thin
Salt and white pepper to taste
2 medium-size Roma tomatoes, trimmed and cut into ¼-inch dice
¼ cup red bell pepper, trimmed, seeded, and minced
¼ cup yellow bell pepper, trimmed, seeded, and minced
¼ cup red onion, peeled and minced
3 tablespoons capers
12 Kalamata olives, sliced
⅓ cup lime juice (about 3 limes)
½ cup olive oil

PREPARATION: Arrange the 'ahi flat on a serving platter. Sprinkle salt and pepper over the 'ahi. Sprinkle the diced and minced vegetables, capers, and olives over the fish. Chill, covered, for about 30 minutes.

When you are ready to serve the carpaccio, bring the platter out of the refrigerator. Sprinkle the lime juice over the fish and drizzle it with the olive oil.

SEARED SASHIMI

These dishes are inspired by Japanese tataki, in which sashimi-grade fish is briefly seared so that the outside is cooked but the inside is still raw, creating a tasty contrast in flavor and texture. Why don't I call these tataki? Because Japanese tataki is a specific dish, served with a specific sauce, and these dishes are in no way regulation tatakis. They are a great introduction to raw fish for those still squeamish. And they are just plain good to eat.

Seared Yellowtail Salad

Serves 4 to 6 as entrée

Hamachi (yellowtail) is in great demand for sushi and sashimi, thanks to its wonderful flavor and fine texture. It is expensive, but so versatile that it is worth the price. In this recipe, I surround the fish with ingredients that enhance but do not overwhelm its taste. The yellowtail takes center stage.

> 2 pounds sashimi-grade yellowtail, cut into ¾-inch dice
> 4 average-size tomatoes, trimmed and chopped
> ¼ cup green onion, chopped
> ½ cup cilantro, chopped
> ½ cup fresh basil, minced
> 2 Hawaiian chili peppers, trimmed and minced
> ¼ cup olive oil (for searing fish)

> ### For the marinade:
> ¼ cup fish sauce
> ½ cup lime juice (about 4 limes)
> 1 tablespoon honey

PREPARATION: Combine the ingredients for the marinade. Marinate the fish in this mixture for at least 1 hour, covered, in the refrigerator.

Put the olive oil in a sauté pan and heat until it is almost smoking hot. Sear the marinated yellowtail cubes; this should take only about a minute. Do not overcook.

While the seared fish is still warm, toss with tomatoes, green onion, cilantro, basil, and chili peppers. Serve at once.

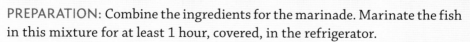

Marinated 'Ahi Salad Crunch

Serves 4 as an appetizer

This dish is a more elaborate version of my signature 'Ahi Poke Salad (see page 35). Some of my customers didn't like eating raw fish, so I created this variation. I marinate the 'ahi and then sear it briefly. The outside of the fish cooks, while the inside remains rare or raw. As in the original, chilled greens, cold noodles, warm fish, and crunchy tortillas make for an interesting contrast of tastes and textures. I've added a medley of crisp garnishes.

If you'd like a low-calorie alternative, simply omit the deep-fried tortillas and in place of the oil in the marinade, use low-calorie, low-fat salad dressing. You can also make this dish with mahimahi rather than 'ahi.

1 pound sashimi-grade 'ahi fillet (each fillet should be about ½ inch thick)
Vegetable oil for searing fish (about 2 tablespoons)
2 cups cooked somen or soba noodles
8 flour tortillas

For the marinade:
1 cup shoyu
½ cup light vegetable oil
¼ cup green onion, finely sliced
2 tablespoons garlic, peeled and minced
2 tablespoons ginger, peeled and minced
1 teaspoon cilantro, minced
1 teaspoon salt
½ teaspoon brown sugar
1 teaspoon Chinese five-spice powder
2 tablespoons kuro goma (black sesame seeds)
Pinch of red chili pepper flakes OR 2 fresh Hawaiian chili peppers, trimmed and minced

For the garnish:
3 cups salad greens, washed, dried, and torn into bite-size pieces
2 carrots, peeled, trimmed, and cut into curls
2 radishes, peeled, trimmed, and cut into curls
2 cucumbers, peeled and cut into long, thin, diagonal slices
2 vine-ripened tomatoes, trimmed and cut into wedges

4 sprigs cilantro
2 teaspoons kuro goma (black sesame seeds)
¼ cup chopped roasted macadamia nuts
Salad dressing of your choice

PREPARATION: Combine all marinade ingredients. Blend well. Remove 2 tablespoons of marinade before marinating fish, and set it aside; you will put this on the noodles later. Marinate 'ahi fillets in the shoyu mixture for 5 minutes, or less, then remove fish and set aside.

Cook somen or soba noodles according to package directions; rinse well in cold water and drain. Take the 2 tablespoons of marinade you set aside and mix it with the noodles. Chill noodles in the refrigerator for 20 to 30 minutes.

Prepare the garnishes. Have everything ready to go before you deep-fry the tortillas and cook the fish. The tortillas must be crisp and the fish must be hot when you serve this. When you have everything ready, heat the oil in a deep-fryer or a large pot to 350°F. Deep-fry the tortillas until they are golden-brown on both sides. Remove and drain on a paper towel.

Heat a flat griddle or a sauté pan over high heat; add the oil, using just enough to cover the bottom of the pan. Sear the marinated 'ahi for about one minute per side. Do not let the fish cook all the way through. You want the fish to remain raw in middle.

Set out 4 serving plates. Put a deep-fried tortilla on each serving plate and arrange the salad greens on top. Place another tortilla on top of the greens. Mound the cooked noodles on the tortilla and put the seared fish on the noodles. Note that this must be done at the last minute. If you put the greens and noodles on the tortilla too soon, it will become soggy.

Scatter a handful of vegetable curls on top of the 'ahi. Add a sprig of cilantro and sprinkle with the black sesame seeds and chopped nuts. Arrange a few slices of cucumber and tomato around the edge of the plate. Drizzle the salad with your favorite salad dressing. For a family-style presentation, spread the greens over a large platter. Mound the noodles in the center. Break the tortillas in half and arrange them around the edge of the platter. Tuck the cucumber and tomatoes between the tortillas. Put the 'ahi on the noodles and sprinkle the vegetable curls, seeds, and macadamia nuts over all. Drizzle with salad dressing.

Ginger-Marinated Seared Sashimi

Serves 8 as appetizer, 2 to 3 as entrée

This dish is deceptively simple. Success depends on the quality of your ingredients and your timing when you cook the fish. If you use sad, wilted vegetables, you'll lose the contrast between the fish and vegetable textures. If you let the fish cook too long, you'll have cooked fish, not seared sashimi. Pay attention to details here and you'll be amply rewarded.

> 2 pounds sashimi-grade 'ahi or swordfish, cut into 2 x 2-inch squares
> ½ cup Ginger Marinade (see recipe on page 135)
> ½ cup Spicy Sashimi Dipping Sauce (see recipe on page 145) OR a sauce of your choice
>
> For the garnish:
> 2 cups cabbage, shredded (Napa, head cabbage, or red cabbage)
> Optional: add sprouts, like assorted microsprouts—broccoli, alfalfa, mung bean, radish (kaiware)
> 2 teaspoons kuro goma (black sesame seeds)

PREPARATION: Prepare the marinade and the dipping sauce, if you don't have any on hand. Marinate 'ahi in the Ginger Marinade for 45 minutes, covered, in refrigerator.

While the 'ahi marinates, you can prepare the shredded cabbage. Remove any wilted leaves, core and quarter, then cut into thin shreds.

After marinating the 'ahi, heat up a hibachi or barbecue grill. When the grill is very hot, sear the fish for 10 seconds or less on every side until all sides are cooked. You can also sear the fish in a very hot skillet, but it won't be as tasty. Slice the fish as thick or as thin as you like.

Spread the shredded cabbage or the sprouts over a serving platter. Arrange the sliced fish on top. Garnish with black sesame seeds and serve with the Spicy Sashimi Dipping Sauce.

Seared 'Ahi with Salade Niçoise

Serves 4 to 6 as appetizer, 2 to 3 as entrée

A niçoise salad typically contains onions, tomatoes, black olives, French beans, tuna, and hard-boiled eggs. This Tahitian variation includes sweet potato, which adds a bit of Polynesian flavor. I've also replaced the tuna with Hawaiian-style seared 'ahi. Three traditions combine to make one delicious dish!

½ pound French beans
2 tablespoons olive oil
1½ pounds sashimi-grade 'ahi (eight 3-ounce steaks)
1 tablespoon cracked black pepper
Salt to taste
½ pound mesclun mix (or any salad greens), washed, dried, and cut into bite-size pieces
2 cups cucumber, peeled, seeded, and julienned into 1-inch matchsticks (about 1 medium European cucumber)
¾ cup red bell pepper, trimmed, seeded, and julienned (about ½ pepper)
¾ cup yellow bell pepper, trimmed, seeded, and julienned (about ½ pepper)
2 cups sweet potatoes, cooked and sliced into ½-inch dice (about 2 potatoes)
1 vine-ripened tomato, cut into wedges
4 hard-boiled eggs for garnish, quartered (optional)
Niçoise olives for garnish (whole or sliced)
¾ cup Soy-Balsamic Vinaigrette (see recipe on page 140)

PREPARATION: Trim the French beans and blanch them for about 2 minutes in boiling water. Remove from the water and submerge in ice water to stop the cooking. Drain and cut into 1-inch lengths.

Heat a skillet over high heat. Lightly oil the tuna and season it with salt and cracked black pepper. Sear 'ahi steaks on both sides, leaving them medium-rare in the center. This should take about 1½ to 2 minutes on each side.

Arrange the mesclun mix on a platter and place the 'ahi steaks on top. Garnish with the French beans, cucumber, bell peppers, sweet potatoes, tomato, eggs, and olives. Serve the Soy-Balsamic Vinaigrette on the side.

Seared 'Ahi with Fresh Vegetable Relish

Serves 3 to 4 as entrée

This dish pairs 'ahi with a vegetable relish inspired by my trips to Jamaica. The relish features fresh tomatoes, cucumbers, onions, and dill—common ingredients in Jamaican cooking. It's moistened with a little rice vinegar and tastes a bit like a sweet vinaigrette. The final ingredient is soba.

4 (6-ounce) 'ahi steaks
8 ounces (1 package) soba noodles

For the marinade:
2 tablespoons rice vinegar
2 tablespoons olive oil
2 tablespoons sugar
¼ teaspoon salt
⅛ teaspoon pepper

For the relish:
1 cup tomato, trimmed and cut into ¼-inch dice
⅔ cup Japanese cucumber, peeled, seeded, and cut into ¼-inch dice
⅓ cup red onion, peeled and cut into ¼-inch dice
1 tablespoon green onion, chopped
1 tablespoon fresh dill, chopped
2 tablespoons rice vinegar

PREPARATION: Boil the soba noodles according to package directions; drain. Combine 2 tablespoons of vinegar, olive oil, sugar, salt, and pepper for the marinade; mix well. Put the 'ahi in the marinade, coat well, cover, and refrigerate up to 1 hour.

Mix the vegetables with 2 tablespoons of rice vinegar and set aside.

Heat a little oil in a sauté pan over high heat. The oil should be close to smoking. Remove the 'ahi from the marinade and sear for about 1 to 2 minutes on each side. Do not overcook. Remove from heat immediately.

For individual servings, divide the cooked noodles among 4 individual serving plates. Put an 'ahi steak on each plate and top with ¼ of the relish.

Cooked Poke

When I'm in the kitchen making poke, or have cut-up fish in front of me ready and waiting for the next step, I just have to experiment. When these experiments succeed, they go on the restaurant menu and into my cooking bible. Here are my most successful ones: flash-fried poke, cooked poke salads, poke patties and sliders, poke laulaus. They show how versatile poke can be. And if poke is getting aged, any leftovers can always be quickly fried in an omelet or served over rice.

Hot Sizzle Wok Poke

Serves 2 to 3 as entrée

Cubed fish is quickly stir-fried and served over crisp lettuce. What makes this dish so good is the complex mix of flavors in the sauce. Besides the usual onion, garlic, ginger, shoyu, and sesame oil (typical of so many stir-fries) I use cilantro and oyster sauce, plus a dash of Sriracha hot sauce for a hot accent. I like to make this in a wok, but if you don't have a wok, a large sauté pan will do.

1 pound ono fillet (or any fresh white fish), cut into ½-inch dice
¾ cup onion, peeled and cut into ¼-inch dice
2 teaspoons garlic, peeled and minced
½ teaspoon ginger, peeled and grated
¼ cup cilantro, chopped
1 tablespoon shoyu
2 teaspoons oyster sauce
1 teaspoon Sriracha hot sauce
1 teaspoon sesame oil
2 tablespoons oil for sautéing
2½ cups mesclun, mixed greens, or lettuce, shredded for garnish

PREPARATION: Mix the ono, onion, garlic, ginger, cilantro, shoyu, oyster sauce, Sriracha sauce, and sesame oil, just as if you were making poke.

Put the 2 tablespoons of cooking oil into a wok or large sauté pan over medium-high heat. Flash-fry the ono poke, then remove immediately from heat. Serve fish on a bed of shredded lettuce, either on individual serving plates or a family-style platter.

Fried A'u Poke

Serves 3 as entrée

An already 'ono a'u poke is seared and served over hot rice. Because the fish isn't completely cooked, you can savor the delicious contrast between the firm outside and the soft interior. Tasty fish juices soak into the rice, so that you can enjoy every last bit of flavor.

1¼ pounds fresh a'u, cut into ¾-inch dice
1 cup ogo, rinsed and chopped
1 cup onion, peeled and chopped
4 teaspoons green onion, chopped
4 teaspoons sesame oil
4 teaspoons shoyu
1 tablespoon canola oil
4 cups HOT cooked rice,
   for serving

PREPARATION: Put the a'u, ogo, onion, green onion, sesame oil, and shoyu in a bowl and mix gently but well.

Heat the canola oil in a wok or sauté pan over high heat. The oil should be close to smoking. Put the fish mixture into the pan and sear for a minute or so. Stir the fish to make sure that all sides of the cubes are seared. Do not overcook. The centers of the a'u cubes should remain raw.

For individual servings, set out 4 serving plates. Divide the cooked rice evenly among the plates. Top with fried a'u poke. For a family-style presentation, spread the rice on a platter and top with the poke.

Fried Poke Mein

Serves 4 to 6 as snack or light meal

Recently, broken saimin has become a popular salad topping. I decided to create a salad using this new technique. This easy and satisfying recipe is just right for anyone looking for a quick snack or a light meal. Remember: just as all poke should be served cold, so should this salad.

1 (2-ounce) package dried saimin (brand and flavor of your choice)
4 cups head cabbage, shredded
1 cup green onion, finely sliced
1 cup roasted almonds or macadamia nuts, chopped
1½ tablespoons sesame seeds, roasted
2½ cups Fried A'u Poke (see recipe on page 82)

For the dressing:
Soup packet from the saimin package
½ cup olive oil or canola oil
3 teaspoons sugar
3 teaspoons sushi vinegar
1 teaspoon sesame oil
Salt and pepper to taste

For garnish:
Fried Wonton Strips (optional) (see recipe on page 103)

PREPARATION: While the saimin is still in the package, break up the dried noodles inside until no pieces are longer than 1 inch. Prepare the Fried A'u Poke and let it cool.

Put the dressing ingredients (soup packet, olive or canola oil, sugar, vinegar, and sesame oil) in a bowl and whisk until thoroughly emulsified. Add salt and pepper to taste.

Put the shredded cabbage, green onion, nuts, sesame seeds, and broken saimin noodles into a large bowl and mix to combine.

Mound the cabbage salad on a decorative serving platter. Pour the dressing over the salad. Arrange the fried poke on top. Garnish with wonton strips if desired.

Layered Tuna Salad

Serves 3 as entrée

This dish is a terrific blend of tastes and textures—crunchy and soft, salty and sweet—it's all here. The vegetables are a riot of color and the Honey-Lime Dressing adds a bright citrus bite.

1½ pound fresh sashimi-grade tuna
Olive oil
½ teaspoon salt
¼ teaspoon pepper
6 ears Kahuku sweet corn
1¼ pounds small purple Okinawan
    sweet potatoes
1 cup fresh cilantro, chopped
½ cup green onion, finely sliced
½ cup red bell pepper, trimmed, seeded, and cut into ¼-inch dice
2 habanero , trimmed and minced
1 cup fresh shiitake mushrooms, sliced
¾ cup Honey Lime Dressing, or to taste (see recipe on page 142)

PREPARATION: Brush tuna with olive oil and season with salt and pepper. Grease the rack of your grill, so that the fish does not stick. Grill over medium heat for about 6 to 8 minutes. Cook until fish is medium; do not overcook. Cool the tuna and cut it into ¾-inch dice. While the grill is still hot, grill the corn. Let it cool and then cut the kernels off the cob.

Peel and slice the sweet potatoes; boil until tender, drain, and set aside to cool.

Put the cilantro, green onion, bell pepper, and habanero pepper in a bowl and mix well. Cover and chill.

Layer the tuna cubes evenly over the bottom of a casserole dish. Drizzle with some of the dressing; be sure to reserve dressing for the remaining layers. Layer the sliced sweet potatoes, shiitake mushrooms, and corn kernels over the fish and drizzle with more dressing; don't use it all. Cover the casserole and chill it for about 1 to 2 hours.

Before serving, sprinkle the cilantro mixture over the casserole of fish, potatoes, and corn. Pour the remaining dressing over the dish. Serve immediately.

Poke Patties

Serves 4 to 6 as entrée

This patty is made from a poke mixture, without any fillers. It's very delicate. I sear it very quickly on both sides, so that the outside is cooked and the inside is still raw. It's like a seared sashimi burger. A tasty mushroom sauce means a little extra work but a whole lot of extra flavor. The recipe calls for 'ahi, but any fish will work well in this dish. Use sashimi-grade fish, since some of it will be raw.

For the patties:

2 pounds 'ahi or aku, minced (makes about 4 cups minced fish)
1 cup onion, peeled and minced
1 cup green onion, minced
½ cup fresh ogo, rinsed and chopped
4 eggs, beaten
½ cup shoyu
1 tablespoon sesame oil
Salt and pepper to taste

For frying:

Panko (packaged Japanese-style fine breadcrumbs) or Italian
    breadcrumbs
4 tablespoons canola oil or as needed

For the sauce:

1 cup mushrooms, thinly sliced
½ cup butter
4 teaspoons shoyu
4 teaspoons oyster
    sauce
4 teaspoons cilantro, chopped

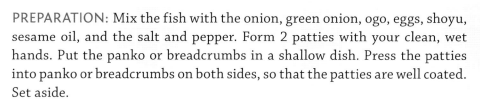

PREPARATION: Mix the fish with the onion, green onion, ogo, eggs, shoyu, sesame oil, and the salt and pepper. Form 2 patties with your clean, wet hands. Put the panko or breadcrumbs in a shallow dish. Press the patties into panko or breadcrumbs on both sides, so that the patties are well coated. Set aside.

Continued on page 86

To make the sauce, sauté the sliced mushrooms in butter for 2 minutes. Add the shoyu, oyster sauce, and cilantro; cook for 1 minute more. Turn off the heat and cover the pan to keep the sauce warm.

Put the oil in a frying pan over medium-high heat. Gently place patties in the pan and brown both sides, keeping the inside of the patties medium-rare.

Pour the sauce over the patties and serve as pūpū, or appetizers.

Buyers inspecting their quarry at a fish auction in Honolulu.

'Ahi-Tofu Burgers

Serves 4 as entrée

Most burgers are made with some sort of filler. Usually, it's breadcrumbs. I like to use tofu. Even after cooking, it stays light and juicy. These patties combine fish and tofu. They're much lighter and lower in fat than beef burgers, and just as tasty.

2 pounds 'ahi
10 ounces (½ block) firm tofu
2 eggs
½ cup fresh shiitake mushrooms, minced
¼ cup onion, peeled and chopped
¼ cup green beans, trimmed and finely chopped
¼ cup carrot, peeled and grated
1 cup soft breadcrumbs
2 tablespoons mayonnaise
2½ tablespoons shoyu
1 teaspoon sugar
⅛ teaspoon pepper
½ teaspoon salt, or to taste
Vegetable oil for cooking

PREPARATION: Mince the 'ahi in a food processor; be careful not to process it into paste. You can also mince it fine with a sharp knife.

Squeeze the excess water from the tofu. One way to do this is to wrap the tofu in a clean kitchen towel, put it on a plate, and put a heavy pan on top of the towel. After about 15 minutes, unwrap the tofu. Crumble the tofu.

Crack the eggs into a small bowl and whisk to combine the yolk and white.

Put all ingredients except the cooking oil in a bowl and mix well. Wash your hands well; leave them wet, so that the mixture doesn't stick to your hands. Hand-shape the mixture into patties. Heat the oil in a skillet or sauté pan over medium heat. Fry the patties on both sides until they are golden brown.

Island-Style Poke Patty

Serves 3 to 4 as light entrée

These 'ahi patties are made with breadcrumbs or panko rather than tofu, and they're flavored with celery and olive oil. Not your usual Island flavors. The patties are different, but delicious in their own way.

1½ pounds 'ahi (makes about 3 cups minced)
½ cup onion, peeled and minced
½ cup celery, minced
¼ cup green onion, chopped
2 eggs, beaten
1 cup panko or breadcrumbs
¼ cup shoyu
2 tablespoons olive oil
1 tablespoon sesame oil
1 teaspoon black pepper
½ teaspoon salt or to taste

PREPARATION: Mince the 'ahi in a food processor; be careful not to process it into paste. You can also mince it fine with a sharp knife.

Mix all ingredients and shape into patties with clean, wet hands. Sauté or grill the patties for about 3 to 4 minutes on each side. Enjoy! Goes great with any of the aiolis on pages 138-139.

'Ahi Cakes with Wasabi Aioli

Makes 8 cakes

I modeled this recipe on the ever-popular crab cake. It differs from a crab cake in that I use less filler and more 'ahi. The flavor of the fish stands out clearly. Mayonnaise adds creamy richness. A drizzle of wasabi aioli is the final touch.

> 1 pound 'ahi
> 2 tablespoons green onion, chopped
> 2 eggs, beaten
> ¼ tablespoon panko
> 3 tablespoons mayonnaise
> ¼ tablespoon shoyu
> 1 teaspoon sesame oil
> ½ teaspoon salt, or to taste
> 4 tablespoons flour, for dredging
> 2 tablespoons light olive oil
> 1 cup Wasabi Aioli (see recipe on page 138)

PREPARATION: Mince the 'ahi in a food processor; be careful not to process it into paste. You can also mince it fine with a sharp knife.

Mix the 'ahi, green onion, eggs, panko, mayonnaise, shoyu, sesame oil, and salt. You will probably want to do this with your clean hands; wet them first, so that the mixture doesn't stick to your hands. Hand-shape the 'ahi mixture into 8 patties.

Dust the patties with flour on both sides. Heat the olive oil in a sauté pan over medium heat. Cook the patties in the oil for approximately 2 minutes on each side, or until the patties are golden-brown. Drizzle with Wasabi Aioli before serving.

Cooked Poke

Salmon Dynamite

Serves 4 to 6 as appetizer

Japanese restaurants use odd bits of seafood to make dynamite: seafood over cooked rice, covered with a mayonnaise sauce, and baked or grilled. It's a handy way to use up bits that would otherwise be wasted.

This is my take on dynamite. No odd bits, just yummy salmon, sliced kamaboko (Japanese fishcake), and other goodies, broiled over cooked rice. You can serve this family-style, as a casserole, or you can serve it as individual portions. Either way, it's easy and good.

1½ pounds salmon, diced (makes about 2 cups diced)
1 cup kamaboko (Japanese fishcake), sliced
2 tablespoons tobiko (flying fish roe)
1 cup button mushrooms, thinly sliced
1½ cups mayonnaise
1 cup sour cream
1 tablespoon shoyu
1 tablespoon sesame oil
1 teaspoon Sriracha hot sauce
3 cups Sushi Rice (see recipe on page 101) or cooked rice
1½ tablespoons furikake (use your favorite)
2 tablespoons or more Honey Wasabi Aioli (see recipe on page 138)

For the garnish:
2 (1.8-ounce) packages Korean nori

PREPARATION: Put the salmon, kamaboko, tobiko, mushrooms, mayonnaise, sour cream, shoyu, sesame oil, and Sriracha hot sauce in a bowl. Mix well.

Spread the cooked rice evenly over the bottom of a 9 x 13-inch glass baking dish. Sprinkle the rice with furikake. Top with the salmon and kamaboko mixture. Drizzle the Honey Wasabi Aioli on top. Broil for 8 to 10 minutes. The top should be lightly browned.

For individual servings, set out 4 to 6 plates, top each with a 2 x 3-inch sheet of Korean nori, and mound a few spoonfuls of the dynamite on the nori. For a family-style presentation, simply set out the casserole dish and let your family serve themselves.

Potpourri

While these recipes involve poke in one way or another, they're otherwise unclassifiable. What they have in common is that they taste good and show poke's many uses—how diced raw fish can be used in a multitude of ways beyond its original purpose.

Poke Shooter

Makes 4 to 6 shooters

Chefs started making shrimp and lobster shooters, so I thought, "Why not a poke shooter?" The poke and the tomato juice combine for a sweet, savory, and spicy flavor.

½ pound sashimi-grade 'ahi, cut into ¾-inch dice (makes 1 cup diced)
1 tablespoon onion, peeled and minced
½ teaspoon salt
2 vine-ripened tomatoes
Pinch microgreens OR chiffonade basil leaves
½ tablespoon red bell pepper, seeeded and minced
½ tablespoon yellow bell pepper, seeded and minced
1 teaspoon cilantro, chopped
2½ cups tomato juice
1 tablespoon wasabi
1½ tablespoons sugar
½ teaspoon sour cream
½ teaspoon tobiko (flying fish roe)

PREPARATION: Combine the 'ahi, onion, and salt to make the poke.

Remove tomatoes from the vine. Cut an X on the bottom of the tomatoes. Place them in boiling water for 3 to 4 minutes and remove. Immediately submerge them in ice water to stop the cooking. Remove the tomatoes from the ice water and peel them. Cut them in half and squeeze out the seeds. Cut into ¼-inch dice.

If you're using microgreens, wash, dry, and cut into thin shreds. If you want to make the basil chiffonade, stack some basil leaves on top of each other, roll the stack into a cylinder, and slice across the cylinder in slices as thin as you can make them. You'll end up with fine threads of basil.

Mix the diced tomatoes with the red and yellow bell pepper, and cilantro. Set aside. Put the tomato juice, wasabi, and sugar in a blender and blend well. Put 1 teaspoon of poke into a shot class, then add some tomato and bell pepper mixture. Pour the tomato juice and wasabi over the top. Garnish with sour cream first, sprinkle with tobiko, and finish with a pinch of microgreens or chiffonade basil.

Grilled 'Ahi with Lime-Shoyu Marinade

Serves 4 to 6 as appetizer, 2 to 3 as entrée

This 'ahi tastes great made on a standard stove-top grill or broiled under the broiler. However, if you want to experience the full flavor of this dish, load your charcoal grill or hibachi with kiawe charcoal and grill the fillets for about 10 minutes on each side. Tasty marinade and kiawe smoke make this one a block-party favorite.

1½ pounds 'ahi (4, 6-ounce fillets)

Marinade:
2 tablespoons cilantro, chopped
1 tablespoon garlic, peeled and minced
2 teaspoons ginger, peeled and minced
Juice and grated zest of 1 average-size lime
¼ cup canola oil
¼ cup shoyu
2 tablespoons dry sherry
1 tablespoon brown sugar
⅛ teaspoon Chinese five-spice powder

PREPARATION: Mix all the marinade ingredients and add the 'ahi fillets. Refrigerate, covered, for 1 hour, turning occasionally.

Grill or broil fish for 10 to 12 minutes, turning once and basting occasionally with marinade. Do not overcook.

Poke Fried Rice Wrap

Serves 4

Tortilla wraps are one of the latest food trends. I decided to wrap up two of my favorite dishes: poke and Island-style fried rice made with bacon and lup cheong. Crazy idea, but it works. Starting with fresh hot fried rice, the heat from the rice cooks the poke a little, firming up the fish and adding a whole new layer of taste.

It's hard to say just how many tortillas you will need and how many wraps you will make. If you find it difficult to make a fat wrap, you might try making some skinny ones; they are easier to roll up. Buy a whole package of tortillas to be sure that you will have enough. Any spare tortillas can be quick-fried, salted, and served as chips—perhaps with some poke.

> 2⅔ cups prepared poke (any kind)
> 4 or more (10-inch diameter) flour tortillas

> ### For the fried rice:
> 1 cup bacon, sliced into ⅓-inch strips
> 1 cup lup cheong, diced
> 1 cup onion, cut into ¼-inch dice (about 1 small onion)
> ¼ cup green onion, peeled and chopped
> 2½ teaspoons garlic, peeled and minced
> 3½ cups hot cooked rice
> 3 eggs, beaten
> 3½ tablespoons shoyu
> 3 tablespoons oyster sauce
> 1 tablespoon sesame oil
> ¾ teaspoon white pepper

Preparation: Heat a wok or a large sauté pan over medium heat. Add the bacon and cook about 3 to 5 minutes. The bacon should not be completely cooked. Add the lup cheong and cook another 2 minutes. Add the onion, green onion, and garlic and cook until the onions are soft.

Add the rice and stir-fry for about 2 to 3 minutes. Make a hole in the middle of the rice mixture and pour the beaten eggs into the hole. Scramble the eggs in the middle of the pan. When the eggs are cooked, toss to mix the fried rice.

Add the shoyu, oyster sauce, sesame oil, and white pepper and mix again.

Put one of the large tortillas down on the counter and spoon about some fried rice into the center. Add a line of poke on top of the rice. I usually use about 1 cup of fried rice and ⅔ cup of poke for each 10-inch wrap. Shape the filling into a log about 1 or 2 inches wide and perhaps 7 inches long.

Fold the bottom of the tortilla up and over the filling. Fold the sides over towards the center. Finish rolling up the wrap. If you're having a hard time making the wrap, try reducing the amount of fried rice and poke filling. Repeat these steps until you've rolled up all the filling.

Try serving these wraps with one of my aioli sauces (see recipes on pages 138-139) or with your favorite salsa.

A colorful sampling of poke—from Spicy Marlin Poke to Limu Poke.

Sushi Rice

Makes 3 cups

If you don't want to make your own sushi vinegar, you can buy it ready-made at the supermarket.

1½ cups short-grain white rice, cooked
1½ cups water

For the sushi vinegar:
3 tablespoons rice vinegar
1½ tablespoons sugar
½ teaspoon salt

PREPARATION: While the rice is cooking, heat the rice vinegar, sugar, and salt in a small pan until the sugar and salt have completely dissolved. Let the sushi vinegar cool. You can skip this step if you're using ready-made sushi vinegar.

Spread the hot rice evenly over the bottom of a large glass baking pan (or a wooden sushi bucket, if you have one). Slowly pour the sushi vinegar over the hot rice, mixing and turning the rice with a rice paddle. Veteran sushi makers like to fan the sushi as they turn it, to increase the speed of evaporation. You can use a table fan or do this traditional way, with a hand-held fan.

The sushi rice is done when the sushi vinegar has been completely absorbed by the hot rice.

Poke Lumpia

Serves 4 to 6

Got leftover poke? Roll it up in lumpia wrappers and fry it. Simple idea, fantastic results. The frying cooks the poke, and the wrapper keeps all those tasty juices inside its crisp, brown crust.

If you don't have time to fry the poke lumpia right away, you can freeze them after rolling them. Lay them out, separately, on a plate or pan, so that they don't clump together as they freeze. When they're frozen hard, you can store them in a sealed plastic bag. Great for unexpected guests.

> 2 cups of your favorite poke recipe
> 1 pound (1 package) lumpia wrappers
> Vegetable oil for frying
> ¾ cup Sam Choy's Original Asian Creamy Dressing (see recipe on
>   page 143)

PREPARATION: Lumpia wrappers are large and square. Put a wrapper in front of you so that one of the corners is pointing at you. Place about 2 tablespoons of the poke several inches up from that corner. The poke should be arranged in a line about 3 to 4 inches long, you know, lumpia-size.

Now take the corner of the wrapper closest to you and fold it up and over the filling. Fold the right and left corners of the wrapper over towards the center. Roll the lumpia until there's just a bit of wrapper corner left at the top. With a pastry brush or your fingers, brush some water on that last corner of the lumpia. Finish rolling up the lumpia. The water will seal the wrapper to itself.

Keep rolling lumpia until you have used up all the filling or all the wrappers. Any lumpia you don't fry right away can be frozen for later use. You will probably have leftover wrappers; those will keep frozen as well.

You can deep-fry the lumpia in a deep-fryer at 350°F, or you can just heat vegetable oil in a pan and pan-fry the lumpia. Cook until golden brown. Remove the cooked lumpia and place on paper towels to absorb excess oil. Serve with some wasabi or my Asian Creamy Dressing. Oh so 'ono!

Fried Wonton Strips

Makes about 2 cups of strips

If you don't have a deep-fryer, fill a heavy skillet with oil, turn heat to medium-high, and fry the strips in the hot oil. You will have to carefully monitor the strips and the temperature of the oil. If the oil is too hot, the chips will burn; if too cool, they will be greasy and soggy. Adjust heat as necessary. You may need to experiment with just one strip, to check the oil, before you fill the pan. Remove strips from oil and drain on a paper towel.

These strips can be made ahead of time and stored in air-tight plastic bags for up to one week.

> **8 wonton wrappers, cut into ½-inch wide strips**
> **Peanut oil for frying**
> **Salt to taste**

PREPARATION: This is best done in a deep-fryer, if you have one. Fill with the peanut oil and heat to 350°F. Add the strips in a frying basket; do not crowd the oil. Cook until crisp. This may only take 1 minute.

Guest Chefs

In the culinary world, chefs are always helping and learning from each other. We attend each other's fundraisers, where we jointly cook. We make guest appearances at each other's restaurants or on each other's television shows. We're like fraternity brothers and sorority sisters. Here are some great recipes from my fellow chef friends. Please check out their restaurants and their books.

Uhu Poke

This was known around the restaurant as the Palani Vaughan Poke. We developed this recipe a few years ago, when we were doing research for one of our anniversary events, New Wave Luau II. One of our friends, Palani Vaughan, helped us with our research on how the old Hawaiians used fish. In the pre-Captain Cook days, there weren't too many options for seasoning food—just Hawaiian salt, 'inamona, seaweed, and, as in this case, the uhu's fatty liver. We wanted to learn the old Hawaiian dishes as the foundation for a new Hawaiian cuisine.

When I created New Wave Luau I, back when I was at the Mauna Lani, I talked to Danny Akaka Jr. a lot. He taught me this: Before you can make something new, you have to know how to make the old. Know the basics. That's your foundation. So, I say to my team now: "Learn to cook with two feet on the ground."

I haven't given quantities. The old Hawaiians didn't measure; they cooked by eye, touch, smell, and taste. You can learn to do it too.

Whole uhu, blue or red
   in color
Limu kohu to taste
'Inamona to taste
Hawaiian salt to taste

PREPARATION: Scale and gut the uhu, reserving the fish's liver. Fillet the fish, and cut the meat into bite-size cubes. In a bowl, mash the fish's liver to break it up into smaller pieces. Mix in the desired amounts of limu kohu and 'inamona. Toss in the fish, and season with salt to taste. Chill until ready to serve.

Alan Wong

Chef Wong is the chef and owner of Alan Wong's Restaurant and The Pineapple Room. He is the author of *New Wave Luau*, and numerous winner of the Hale 'Āina and 'Ilima Awards for Restaurant of the Year and Best Restaurant, respectively. He has won several national awards and has been recognized by *Bon Appétit* and *Gourmet* magazines as one of the leading chefs in the U.S. He was one of the founding members of the Hawai'i Regional Cuisine movement. He is known for his marriage of different ethnic cooking styles with the finest Island-grown ingredients. He creates local dishes with a contemporary twist.

ʻAhi and Taro Poke

Serves 4 as appetizer

This poke mixes two quintessentially Hawaiian ingredients: fish and taro. Tomato, chilies, ginger juice, citron zest, and capers add spice and complexity. Use a ripe, flavorful tomato. Lehua taro is a traditional Hawaiian variety. If you can't find this, or if you prefer another variety, you can substitute. Buddha's hand citron is valued for its perfumed zest. If you can't find this citron in any of your local stores, you can substitute lemon zest.

6 ounces lehua taro, cooked and cut into ¼-inch dice (approx. 1 cup)
1 tablespoon fresh ginger juice (start with a piece of ginger root about 5 inches long)
6 ounces sashimi-grade ʻahi, cut into ¼-inch dice (approx. 1 cup)
1 teaspoon chives, minced
½ teaspoon zest of Buddha's hand citron
¼ teaspoon red chili pepper flakes
2 tablespoons extra-virgin olive oil
Salt and pepper to taste
¼ cup Tomato-Caper Salsa (see recipe below)

For the Tomato-Caper Salsa:
1 cup ripe tomato, trimmed and cut into ¼-inch dice (approximately 1 large tomato), do not seed
2 shallots, finely chopped
1 tablespoon fresh parsley, chopped
1 tablespoon capers, rinsed
1 tablespoon extra-virgin olive oil
Salt and pepper to taste

For the garnish:
1 tablespoon black tobiko (flying fish roe)
1 tablespoon wasabi tobiko (fish roe flavored with wasabi)
Fried taro chips (optional; use commercial chips or thin-slice and deep-fry your own)

PREPARE THE TARO: If you are starting with raw taro, scrub it and peel it. Raw taro will irritate your hands, so hold it with a paper towel or use rubber gloves.

Cut it into chunks and boil or steam it until tender but not mushy. Drain and let it cool before you dice it.

To make the ginger juice, peel raw ginger with a knife or the blunt edge of a spoon. Grate the ginger on a ceramic ginger grater. Put the grated ginger into a square of cheesecloth and squeeze to extract the juice.

Put the 'ahi, taro, ginger juice, chives, citron zest, and chili flakes in a non-reactive bowl, such as glass or ceramic. Mix gently but thoroughly. Cover and refrigerate until you are ready to serve.

TO MAKE THE SALSA: For once, you do not need to seed the tomato before dicing. You will want all the juicy goodness in the center of the fruit. Peel and chop the shallots. Rinse, trim, and chop the parsley.

Mark Ellman

Mark Ellman and his wife Judy Ellman have lived on Maui for over twenty years, where they have operated a number of successful restaurants and restaurant chains. Chef Ellman currently oversees Maui Tacos, Penne Pasta Café, Mala Ocean Tavern, and Honu Restaurant.

Chef Mark was one of the twelve chefs who, back in the 1980s, started the Hawai'i Regional Cuisine movement. He has always enjoyed making food that infuses the best of our Hawaiian multi-ethnic cuisine with sophisticated flavors and techniques from around the world.

Put the diced tomato, shallots, parsley, capers, and olive oil in a medium-size bowl and mix well. Add salt and pepper to taste. Measure out ¼ cup of salsa and pour over the 'ahi and taro poke; mix gently. Refrigerate any leftover salsa; it will keep for 3 days.

For individual presentations, set out 4 serving plates. Put a 2-inch ring mold in the center of a plate and fill it with ¼ of the poke mix. Press gently so that the poke will keep its shape, but not so hard that the juices run out. Remove the mold. Garnish with 1 teaspoon each of tobiko and wasabi tobiko, placed side by side on the edge of the poke mold. You can add a few taro chips for an extra flourish.

For a family-style presentation, mold the poke in the center of a serving plate. Place alternating dots of tobiko and wasabi tobiko in a circle on top of the poke. You can add a ring of taro chips around the edge if you'd like.

Fresh Hawaiian 'Ahi Yukke

Serves 6 as appetizer

Our sushi chef, Masa Hattori, came up with this Japanese-Korean fusion dish, a winner in one of Sam Choy's poke contests. Easy to make but sure to get a great big "Wow" if served at dinner parties!

"Yukke" is the Japanese version of the Korean "yukhae," a dish like beef tartare served with a spicy sauce. The Yukke Sauce here is inspired by this Japanese-Korean dish.

1½ pounds sashimi-grade 'ahi (about 3 cups diced), trimmed and
  cut it into ¾-inch dice
½ teaspoon sea salt
Fresh ground black pepper, to taste
1½ cups Yukke Sauce (see recipe below)

For the Yukke Sauce:
1½ cups shoyu
1½ cups sugar
½ cup water
1 tablespoon ginger, peeled and finely chopped
½ tablespoon garlic, peeled and chopped
1 teaspoon sambal olek (Southeast Asian chili-garlic sauce
  (optional)
1½ tablespoons sesame oil
1 teaspoon toasted sesame seeds
½ tablespoon fresh lemon juice

For the garnish:
3 teaspoons orange tobiko (flying fish roe)
2 teaspoons fresh chives, cut into 1-inch "sticks"

PREPARATION: Refrigerate the 'ahi for at least 6 hours before serving. Just before serving, take the 'ahi out of the refrigerator and season to taste with salt and pepper.

TO MAKE THE YUKKE SAUCE: Combine the shoyu, sugar, and water; blend until the sugar dissolves. Add the ginger, garlic, sambal olek (if using), sesame oil, sesame seeds, and lemon juice. Mix well. Chill before using. The sauce can be stored in an airtight container in the refrigerator for up to one month. The recipe makes about 3½ cups of sauce; you will not need to use all of it for this dish.

For individual servings, set out 6 small serving plates. Place a 2-inch diameter PVC or stainless steel ring in the center of a plate. Fill with the chopped 'ahi. Top with tobiko and arrange a few chive sticks on top. Remove the mold and spoon ¼ cup Yukke Sauce around the tuna. Repeat until all the plates are complete. Serve immediately.

For a family-style presentation, mound the 'ahi in the center of a serving plate. Arrange the tobiko on top of the poke and scatter the chive sticks around the tobiko. Spoon the Yukke Sauce around the 'ahi.

D. K. Kodama

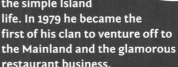

D. K. was born and raised in a family typical of second-generation Japanese in Hawai'i: hard-working parents and six kids happily living the simple Island life. In 1979 he became the first of his clan to venture off to the Mainland and the glamorous restaurant business.

After years spent working in Seattle and Aspen, he returned to the islands and opened his first restaurant in 1996: Sansei Seafood Restaurant & Sushi Bar at Kapalua. He now owns and operates restaurants across Hawai'i. He published a cookbook, *D.K.'s Sushi Chronicles from Hawai'i*, in 2004.

Thai Ribbons

Serves 6

This dish is a fish carpaccio, thinly sliced fish drizzled with oil. The oil is Arbequina olive oil, made from an heirloom variety of Spanish olive. This dish just won't taste the same if you make it with a lesser oil. Green papaya, kaffir lime leaves, and Southeast Asian fish sauce add a tropical touch.

- ½ pound (8 ounces) fillet of sashimi-grade fish, sliced into thin strips
- 2 cups shaved green papaya, shaved into thin ribbons
- 1 tablespoon mint, finely chopped
- 1 tablespoon basil, finely chopped
- 1 tablespoon serrano chili, minced
- 1 tablespoon kaffir lime leaves, minced
- 1 tablespoon fish sauce
- ½ cup Arbequina olive oil

James McDonald

Chef McDonald is currently Executive Chef and partner at Pacific'O, I'o, and The Feast at Lele, on Maui. He trained at the Maui Culinary Institute and apprenticed in Switzerland before returning to the Islands. His restaurants have won too many local awards to list. They achieved national prominence in 2007, when *Gourmet* magazine listed Pacific'O and I'o (combined) as one of the top ten U.S. restaurants with farm connections. (The farm is an 8-acre spread in up-country Maui, where Chef McDonald grows most of the greens, herbs, fruits, and vegetables for the two Lahaina restaurants.) Chef McDonald insists on the best ingredients, cooked with precise technique and displayed with artistic flair.

PREPARATION: Mix all ingredients except the oil. Set out 6 serving plates and divide the fish mixture equally between them. Drizzle the oil over all plates and serve.

'Ahi Tartare Poke

Serves 4 (12 pieces)

This dish was a winner in one of Sam Choy's poke contests. Santa uses some unconventional ingredients, such as daikon and radish sprouts, to make a poke with a bit of bite.

For the poke:
½ pound fresh 'ahi, finely chopped
⅛ cup daikon, finely chopped
⅛ cup Japanese cucumber, peeled, seeded, and finely chopped
2 ounces (½ pack) kaiware (daikon sprouts), finely chopped
½ cup green onion, rinsed, dried, and finely chopped
2 tablespoons fresh cilantro, finely chopped
2 tablespoons garlic, finely chopped
2 tablespoons ginger, peeled and finely chopped
1 tablespoon shichimi togarashi (seven-spice seasoning)
1 teaspoon sesame oil
2 tablespoons shoyu or to taste

For the buns:
1 cup cooked rice

For the Tsume Sauce:
    Makes 2 cups
1 cup shoyu
1 cup sugar
¼ cup cornstarch
¼ cup water

For the Oriental Aioli:
    Makes 1 cup
1 cup mayonnaise
3 tablespoons shoyu
3 tablespoons mirin
1 tablespoon granulated garlic
1 tablespoon black pepper

For the garnish:
½ cup masago (smelt roe)
½ cup shredded nori, cut into
   short 1/16-inch strips

PREPARATION: Combine all the poke ingredients in a large bowl and mix well.

To prepare the Tsume Sauce, dissolve the sugar in the shoyu in a medium-size pot; heat until the mixture boils. Do not use high heat; do not leave unattended. You are making sugar syrup and if you don't pay attention, the syrup will crystallize or burn. Mix the cornstarch and water in a big bowl. The water must be cold, or the cornstarch mixture will become lumpy. Now pour the shoyu-sugar syrup into the cornstarch, stirring as you pour. Keep stirring until the sauce thickens.

Mix the Oriental Aioli in another bowl. All you need to do is mix these ingredients. You will not use all of these sauces, but they will keep for a long time if refrigerated.

Hideaki "Santa" Miyoshi

Santa Miyoshi, co-owner and culinary creator of the popular Japanese izakaya Tokkuri Tei in Honolulu—a bistro chefs and foodies in-the-know often frequent—has twice won first place in the professional class at the prestigious Sam Choy Poke Festival. He is known for his creative, off-the-wall culinary creations. Miyoshi began his culinary career in Tokyo before moving to Honolulu where he ran a Japanese restaurant and then moved on to hone his cutting skills at Kengo's Buffet. Not long after, Miyoshi opened Tokkuri Tei with the help of an investor, where he continues to create a diverse and eclectic menu that combines Japanese, Hawaiian, French, and Italian cooking. The year 2009 marked its twentieth anniversary.

Stuff the cooked rice into a 1½-inch diameter ring mold to make a rice bun; slide the bun out of the mold and repeat until all the rice is molded. Cook the buns on both sides on a grill or non-stick frying pan until the buns are light brown. Set aside.

Put three rice buns on each serving platter. Drizzle the Tsume Sauce and Oriental Aioli over the buns. Put a spoonful of the 'ahi poke mixture on top of each of the buns. Sprinkle masago and shredded nori over the sushi. Serve at once.

There's a Spider In Da Poke
Hideaki "Santa" Miyoshi

Makes 2 rolls (8 pieces)

This is one of the more popular dishes at Santa's izakaya. It combines six different kinds of seafood! If you can't find the Hawaiian Kine 'Ono Drizzle Sauce at the market, you can order it online (several online shops carry it). Ready-made Thai sweet chili sauce is an acceptable substitute.

Santa's sushi-cutting tip: wet your knife. Just let a little water run down the blade and then cut. Repeat as necessary. If you let the knife get sticky, your cuts will be ragged.

1 soft-shell crab (whale size)
Flour for dusting
Vegetable oil for deep frying
¼ cup Maui onion, peeled and thinly sliced
2 tablespoons green onion, rinsed, dried, and finely chopped
2 half-sheets nori
¼ pound 'ahi fillet, sliced ⅛-inch thick
2 ounces hamachi fillet, sliced ⅛-inch thick
2 ounces salmon fillet, sliced ⅛-inch thick
2 ounces (½ pack) kaiware (radish) sprouts, roots trimmed
4 tablespoons Hawaiian Kine 'Ono Drizzle Sauce OR Thai sweet
   chili sauce
2 tablespoons ikura (salmon roe)
2 tablespoons masago (smelt roe)

For the Spicy Ginger Mayonnaise:
2 teasppoons mayonnaise
⅓ teaspoon momiji oroshi (Japanese chili paste) or chili paste of
   choice
⅓ teaspoon ginger, peeled and grated

PREPARATION: Set the deep-fryer to 350°F. Dust soft-shell crab with flour and deep-fry until crispy. It will take about 7 to 8 minutes. Then set aside on a paper towel.

Rinse the Maui onion and green onion under cold water and let them dry. Rinsing onions removes some of the bite. Mix all the ingredients for the Spicy Ginger Mayonnaise.

TO ASSEMBLE ROLL: Place nori on work surface, with the long side facing you. Spread the slices of 'ahi, salmon, and hamachi evenly over the nori, to form one layer of fish. Dab a line of Spicy Ginger Mayonnaise down the middle of the fish layer. Cut the soft-shell crab in half lengthwise. Place the soft-shell crab on top of the spicy ginger mayonnaise. Place kaiware and Maui onion next to soft-shell crab. Roll up like makizushi and set aside.

Cut the roll into 4 pieces with your knife. Place the slices on a plate. Pour 2 tablespoons of Hawaiian Kine Sauce on each slice. If you are using the sweet chili sauce, drizzle sauce to taste. Top with ikura, masago, and sliced green onion. Serve at once.

Guest Chefs

'Ahi Poke

Serves 4 as appetizer

Sam says: This is an old Pang family recipe; Chef Pang got it from his father. I'm thrilled that he was willing to share it with us. It's a simple, straightforward 'ahi poke that is certain to please.

1 pound sashimi-grade ahi, cut into ½-inch dice

½ cup ogo, rinsed and chopped

½ cup Maui onion, peeled and sliced

¼ cup green onion, sliced

1 teaspoon ginger, peeled and minced

1 teaspoon Hawaiian salt or coarse natural sea salt

2 tablespoons shoyu

½ teaspoon turbinado sugar

½ teaspoon 'inamona
   OR ½ teaspoon toasted sesame oil

½ teaspoon red chili pepper flakes

Tylun Pang

Chef Pang is Executive Chef at the Fairmont Kea Lani, on Maui. He's a local boy, born here, and has been cooking since 1974. In 2005, he won the Mayor's Award in Culinary Excellence, Maui County. He currently serves on the advisory board of the Maui Community College Culinary Department. He emphasizes using fresh fish and local ingredients from sustainable resources.

PREPARATION: Cut the fresh 'ahi. Put all the ingredients in a bowl and mix gently but well. Chill, covered, and serve.

Caipirinha-Cured Salmon with Mango-Chili Salsa

Serves 4 as appetizer

What is caipirinha? It's a popular Brazilian cocktail, made with cachaça (liquor from sugarcane), sugar, and lime juice. As it's hard to get real cachaça outside Brazil, I've substituted rum. I marinate the salmon in the caipirinha; the lime in the cocktail "cooks" the fish without heat.

This is a Brazilian twist on the popular ceviche dishes eaten throughout Latin America. This ceviche is complemented by a sweet, hot Mango-Chili Relish. Note that the dish calls for fresh lime juice in the marinade and in the sauce. You'll need to buy at least 3 limes, possibly 4, depending on their size and juiciness.

½ cup lime juice (about 4 limes)
½ cup Brazilian rum (cachaça)
2 tablespoons Malibu rum
6 tablespoons sugar
1 pound fresh salmon, cut into ½-inch dice

For the Mango-Chili Relish:
1 cup red onion, peeled and minced
2 jalapeño peppers, seeded and minced
6 tablespoons water
¼ cup lime juice (about 2 limes)
2 ripe mangoes, peeled and cut into ¼-inch dice
2 tablespoons cilantro, chopped
2 tablespoons mint, chopped

For the garnish:
4 cups blue rock salt
    (see recipe below)
8 fried plantain chips
4 sprigs cilantro

Blue rock salt:
4 cups kosher rock salt
2 tablespoons blue food
    coloring

Place salt in a mixing bowl. Slowly add blue food coloring while mixing. Mix slowly until color is evenly blended.

Jeffrey Mora

Jeffrey Mora has been cooking for than twenty years. He has worked in twenty countries and served as a member of the U.S. Culinary Olympic Team. He is currently the corporate chef and owner of a Los Angeles firm, Metropolitan Culinary Services, Inc. He also serves as chef for the Los Angeles Lakers basketball team.

He is a board member for several environmental groups. He carries his environmental concerns into his menus, which feature meat, seafood, and produce that have been sustainably harvested or grown.

PREPARATION: Put the lime juice, two kinds of rum, and the sugar in a bowl and mix until the sugar is dissolved. Add the salmon and marinate in the refrigerator for 20 minutes.

Put the red onion, jalapeño, and water in a pan and cook over medium-high heat until the water is all gone. Put in a mixing bowl and add the lime juice; mix well. Let sit for 15 minutes in the refrigerator, then add the mango, cilantro, and mint. Mix well.

To make plantain chips, peel one plantain and cut into long thin slices with a mandoline. The slices should be thin, but not too thin to hold together when you deep-fry them. Heat oil in a deep-fryer or a 2-quart saucepan to 350°F. Slip plantain slices into the hot oil by ones or twos; fry for 45 to 60 seconds, remove, and drain on paper towels. Season with sea salt.

Strew the blue rock salt on 4 serving plates and set 4 coconut-shell bowls (or pretty glass or ceramic bowls) on top. Put ¼ of the marinated salmon in each shell. Put ¼ of the mango relish over each salmon serving.

Garnish with plantain chips and cilantro.

Emeril's Poke Salad with Sesame Vinaigrette

Serves 6

Premium ingredients, such as radicchio and sweet onion, perk up this healthy poke salad.

For the poke:
2 pounds sashimi-grade 'ahi fillet, cut into bite-size pieces
½ cup Maui onion, peeled and finely chopped (or other sweet onions, like Vidalia or Walla Walla)
2 tablespoons fresh or reconstituted dried seaweed, coarsely chopped
2 red jalapeño peppers, seeded and minced
3 tablespoons roasted macadamia nuts, crushed

For the vinaigrette:
1 tablespoon garlic, peeled and minced
2 teaspoons shallots, peeled and minced
1 teaspoon fresh cilantro leaves, chopped
¼ cup shoyu
3 tablespoons sesame oil
2 tablespoons kuro goma (black sesame seeds) or regular sesame seeds
2 tablespoons honey
Salt and freshly ground pepper to taste

For the garnish:
1 head radicchio (9 to 10 ounces), washed, trimmed, and julienned
2 teaspoons sesame oil
1 tablespoon fresh chives, snipped

TO PREPARE THE POKE: Put all the ingredients in a bowl and mix gently but well. Cover and refrigerate if not serving immediately.

TO PREPARE THE VINAIGRETTE: Mix the garlic, shallots, cilantro, shoyu, sesame oil, sesame seeds, and honey in a medium-size bowl. Whisk to emulsify. Add salt and pepper to taste. Pour the vinaigrette over the poke mixture and mix gently but well.

TO PREPARE THE GARNISH: Toss radicchio with the 2 teaspoons of sesame oil. Snip the chives into confetti. Arrange the radicchio in the center of a serving platter. Mound the poke in the center and garnish with the chives.

Recipe courtesy of Emeril Lagasse, courtesy of Martha Stewart Living Omnimedia, Inc.

Emeril Lagasse

Chef Emeril Lagasse is a chef, restaurateur, and best-selling cookbook author. He is the chef/proprietor of numerous restaurants in New Orleans, Las Vegas, Florida, and Pennsylvania.

Lagasse is the food correspondent for ABC's *Good Morning America*. He is also the host of cooking shows on the Cooking Channel: *Fresh Food Fast*, *The Originals with Emeril*, and *Emeril's Florida* which premiered its second season in 2014. Lagasse also joined the judges' table on Bravo's *Top Chef: New Orleans*, Season 11 and became Menu Master on TNT's new reality cooking series, *On the Menu* in 2014.

Emeril's Hawaiian-Style Poke
Emeril Lagasse

Serves 4 to 6 as appetizer

Chef Emeril gives Hawaiian poke a new twist with a Southeast Asian peanut butter sauce, also known as satay sauce. Coconut milk and peanuts ... mmmm.

1 pound sashimi-grade 'ahi, cut into ¾-inch dice

For the peanut butter dressing:
½ cup crunchy peanut butter
½ cup coconut milk
1 tablespoon shoyu
2 teaspoons lime juice
2 teaspoons Emeril's Kick It Up Red Pepper Sauce, or hot pepper
   sauce of choice
1 teaspoon sesame oil
¼ cup red onion, peeled and minced
¼ cup green onion, minced (green parts only)
2 teaspoon garlic, peeled and minced

For the garnish:
¾ cup ogo, rinsed and chopped
5 teaspoons roasted peanuts, chopped

PREPARATION: In the bowl of a food processor, combine the peanut butter, coconut milk, shoyu, lime juice, hot sauce, and sesame oil, and process on high speed. Add the red onion, green onion, and garlic, and process until smooth.

Place the 'ahi in a large bowl and toss with the peanut butter dressing. Set out 4 to 6 small serving plates and divide the tuna among them. Top each portion with the chopped seaweed and chopped peanuts, and serve at once.

Recipe courtesy of Emeril Lagasse, courtesy of Martha Stewart Living Omnimedia, Inc.

'Ahi Poke

Serves 4 to 6 as appetizer

'Ahi is cut into bite-size cubes and drizzled with hot oil, partially cooking it. Pickled shallots and a ginger-shoyu-sesame sauce add punch.

- 1 to 1½ pound sashimi-grade 'ahi, cut into ½-inch dice
- ¼ cup pickled rakkyo, thinly sliced (Japanese shallots)
- ¼ cup cilantro, chopped
- 2 teaspoons garlic powder
- 1 teaspoon Hawaiian sea salt
- 1 tablespoon peanut or vegetable oil
- ¾ cup ogo, rinsed and chopped for garnish

For the sauce:
- 6 tablespoons shoyu
- 2 teaspoons ginger, peeled and minced
- 1 tablespoon sesame oil

PREPARATION: Put the 'ahi cubes, rakkyo, cilantro, garlic powder, and salt in a bowl and mix well.

Heat the peanut or vegetable oil in a small pan. It should be very hot, close to smoking. Pour the hot oil over the 'ahi cubes. The oil should be hot enough that the 'ahi sizzles when the oil touches it.

In a separate small bowl mix suace ingredients. Pour the ginger-shoyu-sesame sauce over the fish. Garnish with the ogo and enjoy!

Derek Kurisu

Derek Kurisu is currently the Executive Vice-President at the Big Island's local-grown supermarket chain, KTA Superstores. He has worked for KTA, either part- or full-time, since 1968. He is also extremely active in Big Island community associations and charities.

He will always have a place in the hearts of Hawai'i chefs and consumers for his initiative in creating Mountain Apple Brand products. This is a KTA private label that works with Big Island growers and artisans to bring local foods to supermarket shelves.

Yellowtail Sashimi

Serves 2 to 4 as appetizer

Yellowtail (hamachi) is a delicious fish in great demand for sashimi and sushi. It can be expensive. When you serve it, you want to emphasize it. In this dish, emphasis is added by a crisp fried shallot garnish and a sweet-and-sour shallot dressing. You'll need about 3 shallots for this dish. 2 are fried and 1 is finely minced. Keep this in mind when you're making up your shopping list.

⅓ **pound sashimi-grade yellowtail (hamachi), trimmed, cleaned, and sliced ⅛-inch thick and 2 inches long**

For the garnish:
3 shallots
½ cup canola oil
6 Thai basil leaves
1 teaspoon white ground pepper
Kosher salt

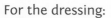

For the dressing:
1½ tablespoons shallots, minced
1 small Thai chili, seeded and finely minced
¼ cup lime juice (about 2 limes)
1 teaspoon white sugar
⅛ teaspoon fresh ground black pepper
Kosher salt to taste

PREPARATION: Peel and thinly slice 2 shallots; the slices should be about 1/8-inch thick.

Chiffonade the basil leaves, that is, stack them up, roll them into a cylinder, and cut the cylinder into slices as thin as you can make them. You'll end up with very thin shreds of basil. Peel the other shallot and mince it fine.

Heat the oil in a small sauce pan until it reaches 325°F. Fry the thin-sliced shallots until they are a light golden-brown. Remove them from the oil with a strainer and put them on a paper towel to cool. Lay them out in a single layer.

Set aside the pan full of oil in which you cooked the shallots. Take out 1 tablespoon of the shallot oil and put it in a small bowl, to cool separately.

Mix the minced shallot, minced Thai chili, lime juice, sugar, black pepper, and salt. Set aside.

Reheat reserved shallot oil (not the cooled single tablespoon) to 300°F and flash-fry the already-golden shallots for 5 to 10 seconds to crisp them; lay on a paper towel again to cool.

Arrange the slices of yellowtail on a large serving plate or individual serving plates. Rub each slice with a little of the cooled shallot oil. Season each piece with kosher salt and white pepper. Drizzle about ⅛ teaspoon of dressing over each slice. Add a pinch of the fried crispy shallots and a pinch of the shredded Thai basil to each piece. Serve immediately.

Charles Phan

The Phan family, originally from Vietnam, immigrated to the U.S. after the Vietnam War. Charles studied architecture at the University of California, Berkeley, and later took over his family's garment business. In the early 1990s, he was drawn into the Internet boom and sold software for a time.

But he never stopped being interested in food. In 1995, backed by his family, he opened a restaurant, The Slanted Door, which served locally-sourced, modern Vietnamese cuisine. It was an immediate hit and has continued so to this day.

Tako Poke

Serves 4

I learned how to make this poke from Ron Shinoda, who graciously gave me permission to share this recipe with you. I've made a few changes here and there, so this may not taste exactly like Ron's poke. I hope you—and Ron—will enjoy the variation. I'm not going to tell you how to clean and cook tako (octopus). I'm assuming that you're buying it already cooked.

½ pound tako, cooked and sliced thin
2 vine-ripened tomatoes, cut into ¼-inch dice
¼ cup Maui onion, peeled and cut into ¼-inch dice
½ cup green onion, chopped
½ cup ogo, rinsed and chopped
⅛ cup limu kohu or līpoa, rinsed and chopped
½ teaspoon 'alaea salt

For the dressing:
¼ cup cider vinegar
¼ cup brown sugar
1 tablespoon sambal oelek (Southeast Asian chili-garlic sauce)
1 teaspoon gochujang (Korean chili paste)

PREPARATION: Put the tako, tomato, onion, green onion, seaweeds, and salt in a large glass or ceramic bowl and mix gently but well.

Put the cider vinegar, brown sugar, sambal oelek, and gochujang in another bowl and mix well. If you're worried that the dressing may be too hot, you can add the sambal oelek and gochujang in increments and taste after every addition. Pour the dressing over the tako poke and mix again. Chill, covered, before serving.

Russell Siu

Russell is co-owner and Executive Chef of 3660 on the Rise. He creates the restaurant's distinctive Euro-Island cuisine, a blend of East and West that uses seasonal products from Hawai'i's oceans and farms.Russell took his first cooking job when he was fifteen. He started from the bottom and worked his way up. He went from cooking at drive-ins, to coffee shops, to restaurants, to international clubs, and finally to opening his own restaurants. He credits his family heritage for fanning his interest in food. His paternal grandfather was a talented Chinese cook. His maternal grandmother was also a good cook, in the local tradition, and taught him dishes he cooks to this day.

Crispy Fried 'Ahi Belly or Fillet

Serves 6 as entrée

Fried 'ahi, seasoned just right, served over warm rice. Ah, heaven!

2 pounds 'ahi belly or fillet
1 teaspoon shoyu
¼ teaspoon Sriracha hot sauce
¼ teaspoon garlic salt
¼ teaspoon black pepper

For serving:
4 cups cooked rice
1 cup furikake (your favorite)
½ cup Maui onion, peeled and finely sliced
½ cup shoyu (optional)
1 teaspoon wasabi paste (S & B brand if available) (optional)
Vegetable oil for frying

PREPARATION: It takes me about 30 to 40 minutes to prepare this dish; it may take you a little longer the first time.

Rinse the 'ahi. Smell to check for freshness. Check it for bones; remove them if you find any. Cut the 'ahi into slices about 2 inches long. Cut with the knife held at a slanting angle. This makes for an appealing presentation. Mix the

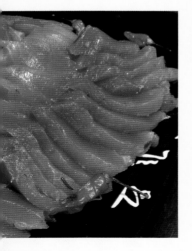

sliced 'ahi, shoyu, Sriracha sauce, garlic salt, and black pepper in a pan or bowl. Set aside to soak for a few minutes.

If you're using shoyu and wasabi, mix them.

Preheat oil in a large nonstick skillet over medium-high heat until hot. Fry the 'ahi slices until golden brown. Do not overcook! Remove them from the oil and drain on paper towels to remove any excess oil.

Spread the rice on a serving platter. Arrange the fried 'ahi on top. Sprinkle with the furikake and sliced Maui onions. Drizzle with the shoyu-wasabi sauce if you'd like. Enjoy!

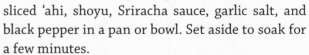

Tanioka's Lomi 'Ahi on Sushi Rice

Serves 4 to 6

We've been serving this lomi 'ahi to delighted customers for more than 30 years. Now you can make it at home, to delight your family and guests.

2 pounds 'ahi or aku, finely
    chopped
2 teaspoons shoyu
½ teaspoon ground chili pepper
    (add more for hotter flavor)
½ teaspoon wasabi paste (S & B
    brand if available)
Pinch of sea salt
4 cups cooked rice or Sushi Rice
    (see recipe on page 101)

For garnish:
¼ cup Maui onion, peeled and
    finely sliced
¼ cup green onion, finely sliced
¼ cup shredded nori
¼ cup salmon roe (optional)
¼ cup tobiko (flying fish roe)
    (optional)

Mel Tanioka

In 1978, Mel and Lynn opened Tanioka's Fish Market, Inc. in a thousand-square foot space with four employees serving fresh seafood to the Leeward sector of the island. With the help of family and friends, Tanioka's Seafoods and Catering now owns a seven thousand-square-foot building. The company's one hundred employees provide customers island-wide with fresh seafood and famous catering products. Tanioka's numerous awards includes the U.S. Small Business Award, the University of Hawai'i's Family Business of the Year, Award, and the Pride in Waipahu Award. Tanioka's was recognized as one of Hawai'i's Best by the *Honolulu Star-Bulletin* and has won the Best of the Best Poke, Seafood, Catering, Bento and SPAM® Musubi recognition from the *Honolulu Advertiser*.

PREPARATION: Mix the shoyu, chili pepper, wasabi, and salt and pour the mixture over the fish. Mix gently but well. Peel and slice the onion. Slice the green onion.

Spread the cooked rice (or Sushi Rice) over a serving platter. Dot the 'ahi in little mounds all over the rice. Sprinkle with the chopped onion, green onion, and shredded nori. Sprinkle with salmon roe and tobiko if you wish.

Condiments

Here are some of the ingredients recommended for the recipes in this book—marinades, chili-pepper waters, sauces, and aiolis. Some are useful for other dishes too, so you may want to make extra. Be creative and experiment like I do!

Sam's Special Salt

Makes 2 tablespoons

1 tablespoon Hawaiian salt
1 tablespoon raw brown sugar
⅛ tablespoon coarse-ground black pepper
⅛ teaspoon garlic powder

PREPARATION: Combine and mix well.

Mirepoix Poaching Water

Makes about 6 cups

4 cups water
2 cups white wine
½ cup cilantro, chopped
⅓ cup carrot, peeled and minced
⅓ cup onion, minced
⅓ cup celery, chopped
2 tablespoons lemon juice (about 1 lemon)
1 teaspoon salt
½ teaspoons cracked black pepper

PREPARATION: Put all the ingredients into a large pot and bring to a boil. You can now poach your meat, seafood, or vegetables in the aromatic water.

After you have finished poaching, you can strain the water through a sieve or cheesecloth to remove any solid bits, then freeze it. You can re-use the water 5 or 6 times before the flavors start to degrade.

New Wave Marinade

Makes 1 cup

2 tablespoons green onion, thinly sliced
1 tablespoon garlic, peeled and minced
1 tablespoon ginger, peeled and minced
1½ teaspoons cilantro, minced
½ cup shoyu
¼ cup light vegetable oil
¼ teaspoon sesame oil
2 tablespoons mirin (Japanese sweet rice wine)
1 tablespoon kuro goma (black sesame seeds)
1½ teaspoons brown sugar
½ teaspoon Chinese five-spice powder
Pinch of red chili pepper flakes OR 1 fresh hot chili pepper,
    trimmed and minced
½ teaspoon salt
¼ teaspoon white pepper

PREPARATION: Combine all the ingredients and blend well. This will keep for 1 to 2 months in the refrigerator.

Ginger Marinade

Makes 1/2 cup

2 teaspoons ginger, peeled and minced
2 hot chili peppers, trimmed and minced
½ cup shoyu
1 tablespoon brown sugar
½ teaspoon sesame oil

PREPARATION: Combine all the ingredients and stir until the sugar is completely dissolved. This will keep for 1 to 2 months in the refrigerator.

Sam's Secret Sauce

Makes 2 cups

My secret sauce? Chili-pepper water! This old Island staple is cheap and easy, but good in proportion to its cost.

> 2 cups water
> 2 tablespoons Hawaiian salt
> 2 Hawaiian chili peppers, trimmed and finely chopped

PREPARATION: Combine ingredients and stir until the salt completely dissolves. This will keep for 1 to 2 months in the refrigerator.

'Onolicious Chili-Pepper Water

Makes 4 cups

Great with all kinds of poke. I sprinkle this on salads and add it to stews, fried fish, and grilled steaks.

> 4 cups water
> 2 tablespoons vinegar, rice wine vinegar, or lime juice
> 1½ tablespoons Hawaiian salt
> 4 average-size garlic cloves, minced
> 8 to 10 Hawaiian chili peppers, trimmed and minced

PREPARATION: Put the water, vinegar or lime juice, salt, garlic, and chili peppers into a medium-size pot. Bring to a boil, then reduce the heat and simmer for about 30 to 45 minutes. Remove from heat and let cool.

You can pour your Chili-Pepper Water into bottles as is, or you can blend it in the blender and then bottle it. This will keep for 1 to 2 months in the refrigerator.

Condiments

'Onolicious Tomato Chili-Pepper Water

Makes 1 cup

1 cup tomato juice
4 tablespoons 'Onolicious Chili-Pepper Water (see recipe on page 136)

PREPARATION: Pour 1 cup tomato juice into a small bowl; add the 'Onolicious Chili-Pepper Water and mix well. This will keep for 1–2 months in the refrigerator.

Hot Ginger-Pepper Oil

Makes 3/4 cup

¾ cup canola oil
¼ cup ginger, peeled and minced
¼ cup shallots or green onion, minced
¼ cup cilantro, lightly packed minced
½ teaspoon red chili pepper flakes
¼ teaspoon salt
⅛ teaspoon white pepper

PREPARATION: Heat the canola oil in a small saucepan until it just starts to smoke. Remove from heat. Stir in the ginger, shallots, cilantro, chili pepper flakes, salt, and white pepper. Let sit until oil is just warm. Strain the oil, discarding the solids and leaving only the hot and spicy oil. Serve hot.

This will keep for 1 to 2 months in the refrigerator.

Wasabi Aioli

Makes 1½ cups

Great with seared sashimi or citrus poke.

> 1½ cups mayonnaise
> 1½ tablespoons wasabi powder
> ½ tablespoon pickled ginger (sushi ginger), peeled and minced
> 1 teaspoon sesame seed oil OR 1 teaspoon wasabi oil
> Salt to taste

PREPARATION: Blend all the ingredients well and chill. This aioli will keep for 1 to 2 months in the refrigerator.

Honey Wasabi Aioli

Makes 1½ cups

Great for salads or sashimi.

> 1½ cup mayonnaise
> 2 tablespoons honey
> 1½ tablespoons wasabi powder
> 1 tablespoon sesame oil
> 1 tablespoon sesame seeds (black or white)
> 1 teaspoon shoyu

PREPARATION: Blend all the ingredients. Refrigerate. This will keep for 1 to 2 months in the refrigerator.

Spicy Honey Aioli

Makes 2½ cups

  2 cups mayonnaise
  2 tablespoons honey
  1½ tablespoons Sriracha hot sauce
  1 tablespoon sesame oil
  1 tablespoon shoyu

PREPARATION: Combine all the ingredients and mix well. This aioli should keep for 1 to 2 months in the refrigerator.

Oriental Citrus Vinaigrette

Makes 2 cups

  ½ cup orange juice
  1 tablespoon fresh basil leaves, chopped
  1 tablespoon fresh cilantro, chopped
  ½ cup balsamic vinegar
  1 tablespoon granulated sugar
  ½ teaspoon dry mustard
  1 cup light olive oil
  Salt and pepper to taste

PREPARATION: Mix all the ingredients, except oil, in a large bowl. Whisk until the sugar is completely dissolved and the mixture is thoroughly blended. Gradually add the oil while continuing to whisk. Readjust the seasoning with salt, pepper, and sugar.

You will not get the true taste of this dressing unless all the sugar is dissolved. Keep whisking until you no longer see any grains of sugar. This will keep for 1 to 2 months in the refrigerator.

Soy-Balsamic Vinaigrette

Makes 1½ cups

   2 teaspoons orange zest
   ½ cup olive oil
   1½ tablespoons shallots, trimmed, peeled, and minced
   ½ cup orange juice
   2 tablespoons balsamic vinegar
   2 tablespoons shoyu
   2 tablespoons honey
   1 tablespoon lemon juice
   2 teaspoons Dijon mustard
   Salt and pepper to taste

PREPARATION: This dressing tastes best when it is made with freshly squeezed orange juice. Before you squeeze, scrape the orange skin with a zester, vegetable peeler, or microplane to get the orange rind. Chop the rind so that you have minced rind rather than long strands. Now you can squeeze the oranges!

Heat a few teaspoons of olive oil in a sauté pan over medium heat. Add the minced shallots and sweat them, that is, cook them until they are translucent, without browning them. You'll have to keep an eye on them; stir and adjust the heat as necessary.

Put the orange juice, orange zest, sweated shallots, balsamic vinegar, shoyu, honey, lemon juice, and Dijon mustard in a medium-size bowl. Mix. Then add the olive oil in a slow, steady stream, whisking as you pour, to emulsify the dressing. Season with salt and pepper to taste.

This will keep for 1 to 2 months in the refrigerator.

Sweet-and-Sour Vinaigrette

Makes about 2½ cups

½ cup carrot, peeled and grated
½ cup cucumber, peeled, seeded, and diced
½ tablespoon ginger, peeled and grated
1 Hawaiian chili pepper, trimmed and minced
1 cup white vinegar
¾ cup sugar
½ cup water
Pinch of salt

PREPARATION: Put all the ingredients into a bowl and whisk until the sugar dissolves. Chill after mixing. This will keep for 1 to 2 months in the refrigerator.

Honey Miso Vinaigrette

Makes 1½ cups

¼ cup green onion, chopped
½ cup white miso (shiro miso)
1 tablespoon sake
1 teaspoon sesame oil
1 tablespoon honey
1 tablespoon vinegar
1 tablespoon sesame seeds
1 teaspoon raw sugar

PREPARATION: Combine all the ingredients and mix well. This will keep for 1 to 2 months in the refrigerator.

Honey Lime Dressing

Makes 1 cup

        ½ cup lime juice (about 4 limes)
        3 to 4 teaspoons lime zest, minced (about 2 limes)
        3 teaspoons garlic, peeled and crushed
        ¼ cup olive oil
        2½ tablespoons honey
        1 tablespoon Dijon mustard
        1 teaspoon salt
        ½ teaspoon black pepper

PREPARATION: Mix all the ingredients and chill. This will keep for 1 to 2 months in the refrigerator.

Creamy Peanut Dressing

Makes 1½ cups

        2 tablespoons cilantro, minced
        1 teaspoon garlic, peeled and crushed
        ½ cup warm water
        ½ cup creamy peanut butter
        ¼ cup vegetable oil
        ¼ cup granulated sugar
        2 tablespoons honey
        2 tablespoons shoyu
        1½ tablespoons rice vinegar
        1½ teaspoons sambal oelek
            (Southeast Asian chili-garlic sauce)
        ½ teaspoon salt

PREPARATION: Mix the water and peanut butter in a small bowl until smooth. Add the remaining ingredients and mix well. Let stand at room temperature at least 30 minutes. This will keep for 1 to 2 months in the refrigerator.

Sam Choy's Original Asian Creamy Dressing

Makes 2 cups

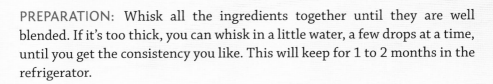

1½ cups mayonnaise
⅓ cup granulated sugar
¼ cup shoyu
¾ tablespoon kuro goma (black sesame seeds)
½ tablespoon sesame oil
⅛ teaspoon white pepper
1 tablespoon water (to adjust thickness)

PREPARATION: Whisk all the ingredients together until they are well blended. If it's too thick, you can whisk in a little water, a few drops at a time, until you get the consistency you like. This will keep for 1 to 2 months in the refrigerator.

Simple Teriyaki Sauce

Makes about 2 cups

2-inch piece of ginger, peeled and grated
3 average-size garlic cloves, peeled and crushed or minced
1 cup shoyu
1 cup granulated sugar
1 cup water
1 tablespoon peanut oil

PREPARATION: Put all the ingredients into a saucepan and bring to a boil. Cool and bottle. Keeps for several months.

Gochujang Sauce

Makes about 3/4 cup

I serve this with tofu and many deep-fried dishes. It's hot and intense.

2 tablespoons green onion, chopped
2 tablespoons roasted sesame seeds, crushed
½ cup gochujang sauce
1 tablespoon sugar
½ tablespoon shoyu
¼ tablespoon vinegar

PREPARATION: Combine all the ingredients and mix well. This will keep for 1 to 2 months in the refrigerator.

Captain Marlin Parker and crew doing tag and release with a marlin.

Spicy Sashimi Dipping Sauce

Makes 1½ cups

This dressing will not taste right if you make it with black pepper instead of white. Don't substitute!

½ cup cilantro, chopped
¼ cup ginger, peeled and minced
¼ cup green onion, peeled and minced
1½ teaspoons garlic, peeled and minced
½ cup light vegetable oil
1 teaspoon red chili pepper flakes
Salt and white pepper to taste

PREPARATION: Put all the ingredients in a blender and blend for 30 seconds. Adjust the seasoning with salt and white pepper. When I serve this with sashimi, I pour it into serving bowls or small individual dipping containers. This will keep for 1 to 2 months in the refrigerator.

The crew of the Magic Marlin II *pose with Sam Choy and his son Sam, Jr. (on Sam's left). From left: Tim Robinson, Jason Holtz, John Patterson, Dave Schatter, Carol Lynn, and Captain Marlin Parker.*

Poke on the Road

"When we first rolled out our poke trucks, we were overwhelmed with the response not just from the local transplants familiar with poke but with nonlocals savoring it for the first time."
—Sam Choy

Poke went on the road in 2013 when I teamed up with Seattle chef Max Heigh to roll out food trucks called Poke to the Max. The Seattle area has a large contingent of former Hawai'i residents who kept asking during my appearances there when poke would be available. Sandwich wraps, rice bowls, and poke salad bowls quickly became standard fare at the food truck as well as local favorites like loco moco,

kālua pork sandwiches, katsu chicken, and popcorn shrimp. Plans are to have trucks roll out in other West Coast cities.

Poke's popularity beyond Hawai'i's shores isn't unexpected as it had become a standard appetizer in many fine restaurants throughout the mainland. This wasn't surprising as many major mainland chefs visited the islands either to work or to appear at food events and tasted local dishes. Additionally, local chefs who were invited to the mainland for assignments and demonstrations would often prepare poke. It would take longer for poke to really go "on the road" and be available for the average person who didn't patronize fancy restaurants. The migration of locals—those born in the islands—to places like Las Vegas, Portland, Seattle, Los Angeles, and San Francisco created a demand for local-style foods. Poke quickly caught on with mainlanders.

Given its ease in making—simply add basic ingredients to taste and additional ones to be creative—poke has become Hawai'i's new export of choice following the hula, the aloha spirit, the 'ukulele, and of course, athletes.

Roasted Sesame Seed 'Ahi Poke

Serves 4 to 6

> 2 cups cubed 'ahi (poke cut)
> ½ cup chopped green onions
> ¼ cup minced onions
> 3½ tablespoons shoyu
> 1⅓ tablespoons hot chili oil
> 1½ tablespoons sesame oil
> 1½ tablespoons toast sesame seeds

Cut 'ahi into ½-inch cubes. Place in a mixing bowl then add all the ingredients. Mix well and chill. Serve about 3 ½ cups of poke on hot rice.

Hawaiian-Style Poke 'Ahi or Aku

Serves 4 to 6

> 1½ cup of cubed 'ahi or aku (½-inch cubes)
> 1½ teaspoons 'inamona
> 2 ounces limu kohu or ogo (seaweed)
> 2 stocks green onions, finely chopped
> ½ or 1 teaspoon Hawaiian salt

In a mixing bowl, add 'ahi or aku, 'inamona, seaweed, green onions, then add salt and mix well. Refrigerate until really cold.

Puhole (Fern Shoots) Poke Salad

Serves 4 to 6

3 pounds fresh fern shoots (in Hawai'i, Waipi'o Valley puhole or
 pohole fern shoots, also known as hō'i'o; best source is local
 farmers market)
2 medium tomatoes, sliced
1 medium sweet onion, sliced
1 cup salted cod fish, soaked and shredded
½ cup cider
1 cup sugar
1 teaspoon grated ginger
pinch of salt
½ teaspoon black pepper

Wash fern shoots and cut or break into 2-inch pieces. To process fern shoots, bring water to boil in a medium pot and drop fern shoots in for 2 to 3 minutes, then place them in a water ice bath and chill. Drain dry.

Then in a large mixing bowl add fern shoots, tomatoes, onion, shredded cod fish, and toss in a mixing bowl.

In a dressing bottle, add cider, sugar, ginger, salt, pepper, and shake very well. Pour all over the fern shoot salad and serve cold.

Poke on the Road

Hawaiian Chili Water—A Must for Poke

Serves 4 to 6

    1½ or 2 tablespoons sea salt
    4 fresh cloves of garlic, minced
    4 Hawaiian chili peppers (bird peppers), minced
    2 cups boiling water
    ⅓ cup vinegar

Mash together salt, garlic, and Hawaiian peppers. Add to 2 cups of boiling water and vinegar and simmer for 10 minutes. Cool and store in a glass jar in the refrigerator. Goes with all poke, salads, and poke rice bowls.

Famous 'Ahi Poke Salad

Serves 4 to 6

    1 pound 'ahi, cut into poke cubes (about ¾-inch dice)
    1 cup assorted cherry tomatoes, cut in half
    ½ cup shelled edamame
    ½ cup minced onions
    ¼ cup chopped green onions
    1 tablespoon sesame oil
    1 or 2 fresh
      Hawaiian chili
      peppers, minced
      (¼ teaspoon chili
      flakes can be
      substuited)
    1 cup diced
      cucumber
    ½ cup chopped ogo

Combine all ingredients in a large mixing bowl. Mix well and refrigerate.

Three Limu Poke

Serves 4 to 6

2 pounds fresh 'ahi, cut into ¾ cubes
¼ cups ogo
¼ cup limu kohu
¼ cup Japanese prepared sea salad

½ cup minced onions
2 Hawaiian chili peppers, minced (substitute with ⅓ teaspoon chili flakes)
½ cup green onions, chopped
3 tablespoons shoyu
1 ½ tablespoons seasame oil
1 teaspoon sea salt

Put all ingredients in a mixing bowl and mix well. Serve cold

Spicy 'Ahi Poke

Serves 4 to 6

2 pounds 'ahi, cubed small
½ cup minced onions
¼ cup chopped green onions
¾ cup mayonnaise
2 tablespoons tobiko (orange fish eggs)
½ cup shredded imitation crab meat
2 tablespoons chili oil
1 tablespoon Sriracha hot chili sauce
4 tablespoons shoyu

Combine all ingredients in a mixing bowl and mix well. Chill, then serve on hot rice or shredded cabbage.

Cucumber 'Ahi Poke

Serves 4 to 6

    2 pounds 'ahi, cut into ¾-inch cubes
    3 cups peeled and cubed (¾-inch) cucumber
    ½ cup minced onions
    1 cup chopped ogo
    ½ cup chopped green onions
    4 tablespoons shoyu
    1 tablespoon seasame oil
    1 tablespoon gochujang sauce
    2 whole chili peppers, minced

In a mixing bowl add all ingredients and gently mix. Chill and serve.

Dried 'Ahi Poke (Good with Beer)

Serves 4 to 6

    3 pounds dried 'ahi, cut into small cubes (to make your own dried
       'ahi, cut fresh 'ahi into ¾-inch cubes, lightly salt, and dehydrate)
    ½ cup seasame oil
    2 tablespoons shoyu
    ½ cup ogo
    1 cup minced sweet onions
    4 Hawaiian
       chili
       peppers,
       minced
    ½ cup
       chopped
       green
       onions

In a mixing bowl,
add all ingredients
and mix well.

Mediterranean Garlic Poke

Serves 4 to 6

3 tablespoons olive oil
1 whole garlic, minced and deep fried until golden brown
3 pounds fresh 'ahi, cut into 3/4 cubes
1 cup minced onions
½ cup minced sweet red bell peppers
½ cup sweet yellow bell peppers
1½ tablespoons shoyu
1 tablespoon sesame oil
2 minced Hawaiian chili peppers
1 cup chopped ogo
½ teaspoon sea salt

In a medium skillet, add oil and deep fry minced garlic until golden brown. Let cool. Then in a mixing bowl, add the rest of the ingredients and gently mix well. Great with chips, crackers, or lettuce wraps.

Furikake 'Ahi Poke to the Max

Serves 4 to 6

2 pounds 'ahi, cut into ¾-inch cubes
1 cup chopped ogo
½ cup minced onions
¼ cup chopped green onions
1½ tablespoons sugar
3 tablespoons shoyu
3 tablespoons sesame oil
2 whole Hawaiian chili peppers, minced
½ cup furikake seasoning

In a medium mixing bowl, put all ingredients and gently mix. Chill.

Tastes great with rice.

'Ahi with Roasted Sesame Seeds

Serves 4 to 6

3 pounds fresh 'ahi, cut into ¾-inch cubes
½ cup minced onions
½ cup chopped onions
½ cup chopped ogo
2 cups cubed avocado (¾-inch cubes)
1 tablespoon oyster sauce
1 tablespoon sriracha sauce
1 tablespoon sesame seed oil
2 tablespoons roasted sesame seeds

Mix all ingredients in a bowl and serve chilled. Great with beer.

Soba and Poke and Avocado

Serves 4 to 6

3 pounds fresh 'ahi cut into ¾-inch cubes
2 medium vine ripe tomatoes, cut into ¾-inch cubes
½ cup diced onions
¼ cup chopped green onions
1 cup chopped ogo
4 tablespoons shoyu

2 tablespoons sesame oil
2 Hawaiian chili peppers, minced
1 medium ripe avocado, cut into
¾-inch cubes
2 bundles cooked soba

In a mixing bowl put all ingredients and gently mix. Chill and set aside. Arrange soba noodles on a bed of lettuce then top off with a cup of poke.

Poke Slider

Serves 4 to 6

    2 pounds fresh 'ahi cut into small cubes
    ⅓ cup minced onions
    ⅓ cup chopped green onions
    1 ripe avocado, mashed really well
    4 tablespoons shoyu
    3 tablespoons sesame oil
    8 sweet slider rolls, cut in half
    2 tablespoons sriracha sacue
    3 tablespoons mayonnaise

Mix all ingredients in mixing bowl and make sure the avocado is really creamy. Spoon a teaspoon of the poke onto the slider bun and serve.

Fast Poke with Magic Poke Sauce

Serves 4 to 6

    2 cups shoyu
    1 cup sesame oil
    2 tablespoons sugar
    2 or 3 whole Hawaiian chili peppers, minced
    2 tablespoons very fine minced onions
    2 tablespoons chopped green onions
    1 mason jar (make sure you have enough room to shake and pour
        all ingredients)

Put all ingredients in the mason jar and shake well. Chill.

When you make any kind of poke, all you have to do is add this magic poke sauce and enjoy. You can mix it with 'ahi, salmon, ono, tomatoes, or avocado, or even use it as a salad dressing.

Glossary & Substitutions

(If not indicated, there is no suitable substitute.)

'A'ama crab: Hawaiian name for the thin-shelled rock crab. It is greenish-black and marked with faint striations; it grows as large as 3 inches across. Scientific name: *Grapsus tenuicrustatus*.

Abalone: A large "ear-shaped" marine gastropod mollusk with a single shell. We usually eat the large muscle. It can be tough, so is often tenderized by pounding or by long cooking. There are about 100 species of abalone, all in the genus *Haliotis*. Substitute frozen or canned abalone.

'Ahi: Hawaiian name for yellowfin or bigeye tuna. Also called shibi in Japanese. Substitute fresh blackfin or bluefin tuna.

Aïoli: GARLIC mayonnaise. Also spelled aïoli.

Ake: Hawaiian word for liver.

Aku: Hawaiian word for skipjack or bonito tuna. Substitute any tuna.

Al dente: Italian term for foods such as pasta and vegetables that have been cooked just to the point that they still offer a slight resistance to the bite.

'Alaea salt: Hawaiian name for a red-tinged sea salt. Iron-rich "red dirt" gives it its color. Substitute sea salt.

A'u: Hawaiian name for marlin, a large game fish with a long swordlike snout. Also known by its Japanese name, nairagi. Use other firm white fish like sea bass, ONO (wahoo), MAHIMAHI.

Baby lū'au: A party for family and friends, held in honor of a baby's first birthday. A tradition in the Islands.

Balsamic vinegar: Vinegar, originally Italian, made from white grape juice and aged in wooden barrels for a period of years. It is very dark and flavorful, having absorbed some of the flavor from the wood of the barrels. Substitute sherry vinegar.

Banana leaves: Throughout the South Pacific, leaves from the banana tree are used to wrap food that will be cooked in the earth oven (see IMU). Available in Asian markets and florist shops. Substitute aluminum foil or parchment paper to wrap food; corn husks (as food wrapper or to cover imus); hoja santa leaves (as a food wrapper, also imparts an interesting anise flavor); or TI LEAVES.

Basil: A fresh or dried herb available in a variety of types including common sweet basil, opal basil, and THAI BASIL. These varieties can be used interchangeably.

Bean sprouts: Usually refers to sprouted mung beans; however soybeans, lentils, and sometimes other beans are used in sprouted form. Generally consumed raw or lightly stir-fried. Substitute canned mung beans or bean sprouts.

Beefsteak tomatoes: Substitute 1½ to 2 cups chopped tomato per beefsteak tomato.

Big Island: Nickname for Hawai'i island, also called the Island of Hawai'i, the largest and southernmost island in the Hawaiian chain.

Billfish: Substitute broadbill swordfish, Pacific blue marlin, black marlin, sailfish, striped marlin.

Black beans: Substitute other firm beans.

Bonito: Dried tuna shavings. Used to make the Japanese broth called DASHI.

Button mushrooms: Small, young, cultivated white mushrooms. Available canned or bottled in most supermarkets. Substitute any other mushroom.

Calamansi: Refers to the low-acid Filipino lemon, which is about the size of a large olive. Substitute lemons or limes.

Calamari: Another name for SQUID. From the Italian. Often used in recipes derived from Mediterranean cuisines. Substitute octopus.

Capers: The flower bud of a bush native to the Mediterranean. Sold dry or bottled in "brine." Always rinse before using to remove excess salt. Substitute chopped green olives.

Carpaccio: An Italian-style dish of raw meat or fish; usually made with beef, olive oil, and lemon juice, and topped with CAPERS and onions.

Ceviche: A method of "cooking" fish with the acid in lemon or lime juices. The acid coagulates the proteins in the flesh.

Chili oil: Vegetable oil flavored with hot chili peppers. This can be purchased in Asian markets. It should be kept refrigerated once opened. Substitute any vegetable oil with hot chili peppers added to taste.

Chili paste: Pastes vary in composition, but generally include hot red chilies, vinegar, salt, and possibly GARLIC. Substitute ground garlic cloves, red chili peppers, onions, and sugar.

Chinese five-spice powder: A fragrant, spicy, and slightly sweet Chinese spice mixture made from ground star anise, Szechuan peppercorns, fennel seeds, cloves, and cinnamon. Substitute 1 teaspoon each ground star anise, fennel seed, and Szechuan pepper plus ½ teaspoon each ground cinnamon and cloves.

Cilantro: Also called Chinese parsley. The green leaves and stems of the CORIANDER plant. Substitute parsley.

Clams: A variety of bivalve mollusks. Sold fresh (either shelled or unshelled), fresh-frozen, or canned. When buying unshelled clams, make sure they are still alive. The shells of live mollusks are tightly sealed, or will close slowly when tapped. Choose clams that have a fresh smell, and avoid those that smell of ammonia.

Clam juice: The seasoned juices of cooked clams. Available canned in supermarkets.

Clam meat: Cooked canned meat from clams in cooking juices. Available in supermarkets.

Coconut milk: The rich, creamy liquid extracted by squeezing the grated meat of a coconut. Available fresh, canned, or frozen in most supermarkets and in Asian and specialty markets. Substitute: (thin) use 1 cup whole milk beaten with 1 teaspoon coconut flavoring; (thick) use 1 cup heavy cream with 1 teaspoon coconut flavoring.

Coriander (seeds): Seeds of the coriander plant. Closely related to caraway, fennel, dill, and anise. Sold in the spice section of most supermarkets.

Coriander (ground): A powder made from the ground seeds of the coriander plant. Available in the spice section of supermarkets. Coriander leaf is also known as CILANTRO, or Chinese parsley.

Crab: Decapod crustaceans; they generally have no tail, or a short tail, and two large claws. Close to 7,000 species of crabs are known. Humans eat many of them. Hawai'i crab varieties include 'A'AMA, KONA, and KUHONU. Often bought live, as that is the only way to be sure that they are fresh. Supermarkets also carry frozen or canned crabmeat.

Cucumber: The fruit of a plant in the gourd family; related to squash and melons. Cucumbers are widely grown and available in many varieties. In Island markets, the long, thin Japanese cucumber and the common garden cucumber are most often seen. Common cucumbers must be seeded; Japanese cucumbers do not need seeding. The English cucumber and the Persian cucumber resemble the Japanese cucumber.

Cumin: The seeds of a flowering plant native to the Mediterranean and Asia. Used as whole seed or as powder. Characteristic of Mexican and Indian cooking. Available in the spice section of supermarkets.

Curry powder: A commercially prepared mixture of spices such as cardamom, chili, cinnamon, cloves, CORIANDER, CUMIN, fennel seeds, fenugreek, mace, nutmeg, red and black pepper, saffron, SESAME SEEDS, tamarind, and turmeric. Different curry powders use different spices in different proportions. Indian cooks usually prefer to mix their own spices. Japanese cooks make great use of commercial curry powders adapted to Japanese tastes. Curry powder can be found in the spice section of most supermarkets. Japanese curry powder may be shelved in the Asian food section.

Daikon: A large Asian radish, usually white in color. Used in Japan and Korea for soups and pickles, or eaten raw. Flavors range from mild to spicy-hot. Available fresh, pickled, or preserved, in most Asian markets. Substitute turnips or radish.

Daikon sprouts: See KAIWARE.

Dashi: A clear, light Japanese fish broth. Sold as instant stock in granules or tea-like bags, or as a concentrate. Substitute chicken stock.

Dill: An aromatic herb with needle-like leaves, small yellow flowers, and pungent flavor. Used fresh or dried.

Dolphinfish: See MAHIMAHI.

Earth oven: See IMU.

Enoki: Small, slim MUSHROOMS. Also known as straw mushrooms. Substitute julienned BUTTON MUSHROOMS.

European cucumber: Also known as "English" or "hothouse" CUCUMBERS. Sold wrapped in plastic in the produce section of most supermarkets. Substitute with other cucumber varieties, e.g., Japanese or Persian cucumbers.

Fish sauce: A concentrated salty brown liquid typically made from anchovies fermented in brine. Used in Southeast Asian cooking. Substitute 1 part SHOYU plus 4 parts mashed anchovies.

Fishcake: White fishmeat ground, shaped, and steamed or baked. A frugal use of the meat from various white fish. Island supermarkets usually carry kamaboko and surimi, Japanese versions of fishcake. Fishcakes are eaten throughout East Asia and Southeast Asia, usually as fish balls. European versions of fishcake, such as the Jewish gefilte fish and the Italian pan pesce, include eggs and breadcrumbs or flour. Substitute mild-flavored white-flesh fish, such as cod.

Furikake: A Japanese condiment made from dried seaweed flakes, SESAME SEEDS, BONITO flakes, sugar, salt, and other seasonings. Available in the Asian section of local supermarkets. Substitute ground sesame seeds and finely chopped NORI seaweed sheets.

Galangal: Two plants in the GINGER family, the greater and lesser galangal. The roots are used in Southeast Asian cooking. Greater galangal is most popular; lesser galangal has a strong flavor that some find too insistent. Substitute ginger root or powdered ginger plus cardamom.

Garlic cloves: Substitute 1 teaspoon chopped garlic or 1/8 teaspoon garlic powder.

Giant trevally: The common English name for a fish, *Caranx ignobilis*, known as ULUA in Hawaiian and Island daily speech. Substitute any crevalle, jack, or pompano game fish.

Ginger: The root of the domestic ginger plant, *Zingiber officinale*. Ginger is used as a seasoning both in savory dishes (typically with GARLIC and SHOYU) and in sweets such as cookies, cakes, and candies. (Powdered ginger is not a good substitute.)

Gochujang: Korean CHILI PASTE. May also contain BLACK BEANS, GARLIC, and spices. Also spelled kochujang. Substitute any chili paste.

Goma: See SESAME SEEDS.

Guava: A sweet, yellow, plum-sized fruit. Substitute LILIKOʻI.

Hagi: Japanese word for triggerfish, brightly colored reef fishes. Islanders usually say "hagi" rather than "triggerfish." All triggerfishes are members of the family Balistidae; there are many genera and species of triggerfishes.

Hawaiian chili pepper: A small, hot chili pepper grown throughout the Islands. Substitute Thai bird chilies or any small hot chili pepper, such as chopped habañero or Scotch bonnet chili pepper.

Hawaiian chili-pepper water: Water infused with chopped HAWAIIAN CHILI PEPPERS; sometimes GARLIC is added. A homemade hot sauce that is very popular in the Islands. Substitute water infused with any hot chili pepper.

Hawaiian salt: Coarse, heavy, white or red crystals made from evaporated seawater. See also 'ALAEA SALT. Substitute KOSHER SALT or sea salt.

He'e: Hawaiian word for octopus. See TAKO.

Hibachi: A small, portable, inexpensive Japanese outdoor grill used widely in backyards, on patios, and at beaches in Hawai'i.

Hoisin sauce: A thick reddish-brown sauce made with fermented soybeans, GARLIC, rice, salt, and sugar. Substitute pureed plum baby food mixed with SHOYU, garlic, and chili peppers.

Hokkigai: Japanese name for surf CLAMS; can substitute frozen or canned clams.

Ika 'ota: Tongan name for ceviche made with raw fish, citrus juice, and coconut milk.

Imu: An underground oven, the earth oven of ancient Hawai'i. A hole is dug in the ground and lined with fire-heated stones. Banana stalks and BANANA LEAVES cover the stones. Often a whole pig is cooked in the imu, together with other meats and vegetables.

'Inamona: Hawaiian word for a relish (in paste or chopped form) made from roasted KUKUI NUTS and salt. Substitute coarsely chopped salted cashew nuts.

Italian parsley: A strong-flavored parsley; also known as flat leaf parsley because of its broad flat leaves. Substitute parsley.

Japanese cucumber: See CUCUMBER. Substitute any cucumber.

Jicama: A large root vegetable with a thin brown skin and crunchy sweet white flesh. Can be eaten raw or cooked. Also known as Mexican potato or Chinese yam. Substitute water chestnuts.

Kaffir lime leaves: Glossy, dark-green leaves used for cooking. They look like two leaves that are joined end to end and have a floral-citrus aroma. Dried kaffir lime leaves can be found in Asian markets. Fresh leaves, which have a more intense, fragrant smell, are sometimes available. Substitute LEMONGRASS or lime zest.

Kaiware: Japanese name for DAIKON radish sprouts. Substitute clover sprouts.

Kajiki: Japanese name for Pacific blue marlin, or A'U. Substitute any BILLFISH.

Kalamata olives: A kind of Greek olive, marinated in brine, with an intense and distinctive taste. Also spelled calamata. Substitute any marinated Greek olive.

Kiawe: A tree that grows abundantly in the Islands. Also known as mesquite. Kiawe wood charcoal is excellent for grilling.

Kimchee: A Korean pickled vegetable usually made with Chinese cabbage (WON BOK), vinegar, salt, GARLIC, and chili peppers. Can be very hot and spicy. Substitute pickled CUCUMBERS or cabbage with garlic and chili peppers.

Kona crab: A long-backed CRAB common in Hawaiian waters. Also known as red frog crab or spanner crab. Open season: September 1 to April 30. Consult Division of Aquatic Resources website (www.hawaii.gov/dlnr/dar). Substitute Dungeness crab or LOBSTER.

Kosher salt: A coarse-grained salt known as kosher salt in the U.S. Used to "kosher" meat by drawing the blood out of it. Substitute coarse-grain sea salt.

Kuhonu crab: A Hawaiian reef CRAB. Also known as white crab. Scientific name: *Portunus sanguinolentus*. Substitute blue pinchers, Dungeness, Australian mud crabs.

Kukui nuts: Hawaiian name for the candlenut. See also 'INAMONA, a relish made with roasted kukui nuts. Substitute roasted cashew nuts.

Kuro goma: Black SESAME SEEDS. Substitute finely chopped toasted almonds.

Laulau: Packages of TI LEAVES or BANANA LEAVES containing pork, beef, salted fish, or TARO tops. Laulaus are baked in an earth oven (IMU) or, more commonly these days, in a regular gas or electric oven. "Lau" means "leaf" in Hawaiian.

Lemongrass: A citrus-scented grass that adds a distinctive lemon flavor and aroma to the cooking of Southeast Asia. Its long, woody stalk grows from a base that resembles the white part of a green onion. Substitute lemon zest.

Li hing powder: A sweet, sour, and salty seasoning traditionally used to make Chinese preserved plums (li hing mui). It is now commonly available as a powder that can be sprinkled on a wide range of foods, giving them the li hing taste that Islanders love. Substitute a mixture of ground dried plum or other fruit, sugar, salt, and sometimes licorice.

Liliko'i: A tangy, plum-sized, multi-seeded tropical fruit. Also known as passion fruit. Sold in frozen concentrate form. Find in the freezer section of supermarkets or Asian markets. Substitute frozen concentrate liliko'i or orange juice.

Limu: Hawaiian word for all types of plants living in the water or damp places. As adopted into English and Hawaiian pidgin, the word now means only edible seaweeds. Substitute seaweeds with similar characteristics like kelp, konbu.

Limu huluhulu waena: An irregularly-branching, dark-red edible seaweed (*Grateloupia filicina*). Substitute kelp.

Limu kohu: An edible red seaweed that may range in color from tan through shades of pink to dark red. Scientific name: *Asparagopsis taxiformis*. Hawaiians consider it a great treat. It is generally rolled into balls and dried after it is collected. Substitute kelp.

Limu līpoa: An edible brown seaweed, generally used in a preserved salted form. Scientific names: *Dictyopteris plagiogramma*, *Dictyopteris australis*. Substitute kelp.

Limu wāwae'iole A dark-green edible seaweed. The name means "rat's foot seaweed." The fronds look somewhat like a rat's foot. Scientific names: *Codium edule* or *Codium reediae*. Substitute kelp.

Lobster: A marine crustacean found in all the world's waters. Dozens of varieties are known; many of these are edible. Specialists divide lobster species into clawed lobsters (like the familiar Maine lobster) and non-clawed lobsters, like the ROCK LOBSTER (also known as spiny lobster) and the slipper lobster. There is a Hawaiian lobster fishery, operating in the waters off the uninhabited Northwest Hawaiian Islands. The local catch is primarily rock lobster and slipper lobster. A Big Island aquaculture company raises Kona lobsters, which are the familiar Maine clawed lobsters. Substitute frozen lobster.

Lomi: Hawaiian and pidgin word meaning to rub or knead. Also known as lomilomi.

Lomi salmon: Hawaiian dish made by mixing chunks of salted raw salmon, tomatoes, and onions.

Long rice: Threadlike noodles made from mung bean flour. Soak in water before cooking. Available in Asian markets, or in the Asian sections of most supermarkets.

Lūʻau: Hawaiian term for a party or gathering. See also BABY LŪʻAU.

Lūʻau leaves: Substitute spinach leaves.

Lumpia: A thin wheat wrapper around a filling, usually composed of minced vegetables, often with bits of meat, seafood, or TOFU. Lumpia are served uncooked or deep-fried. Some deep-fried lumpia are made with a sweet banana filling. Characteristic of Filipino and Indonesian cuisine, they resemble the spring rolls of Southeast Asia.

Lup cheong: Sweet, oily Chinese dried sausage. Available in Asian markets. Substitute Portuguese sausage, anudouille sausage.

Macadamia nuts: Round, oily nuts with a creamy, slightly crunchy texture. Harvested from trees. Most of the world's macadamia nuts are grown on the Big Island. Substitute pine nuts.

Mahimahi: Hawaiian name for dolphinfish. Has firm, light pink flesh. Substitute drum, halibut, cod, seabass, and wahoo.

Makizushi: The familiar cylindrical SUSHI roll. Sushi rice is spread over a sheet of seaweed, topped with various tasty tidbits, and rolled into a cylinder, which is then cut into slices.

Mango: An oval tropical fruit with golden-orange flesh and an enticing, aromatic flavor; skin color ranges from yellow-orange to burgundy to green. Available in the produce sections of Hawaiʻi supermarkets. Substitute peaches or sweet ripe nectarines.

Marlin: See AʻU.

Masago: Capelin (smelt) roe. Eggs of a small fish found in the North Atlantic and Arctic oceans. Substitute fish roe.

Maui onion: A sweet, mild onion, grown in the Kula district of Maui. Substitute Texas, Bermuda, Vidalia, ʻEwa, red, or other sweet onion.

Mesclun: A mix of young salad greens. Often contains dandelion, mizuna, oak leaf, RADICCHIO, and arugula. Available in supermarket produce sections and specialty produce markets.

Mirin: Japanese sweet rice wine. Substitute 1 tablespoon cream SHERRY or sweet vermouth.

Miso: Fermented soybean paste. Substitute condensed chicken broth blended with a small amount of TOFU.

Mushrooms: Mushrooms are the fruiting bodies of fungi. There are thousands of varieties of mushroom, some of which are edible, many of which are not. The most common edible mushrooms have been domesticated and cultivated. The mushrooms commonly seen in Island supermarkets are BUTTON MUSHROOMS, ENOKI, oyster mushrooms, portobello mushrooms, and SHIITAKE MUSHROOMS.

Mussels: Bivalve mollusks. Substitute frozen, previously frozen, or canned.

Mustard: Mustard seeds are harvested and dried and used in cooking. Whole mustard seeds are used in Indian cooking; dry mustard (ground mustard seed) features in some recipes; dry mustard mixed with various liquids or oils makes a condiment (called simply mustard) that comes in many varieties.

Musubi: Cooked rice shaped around a filling (such as a pickled plum or a bit of tuna) and wrapped in a strip of NORI. Hawai'i has developed its own version of musubi, the SPAM® musubi. A slice of fried TERIYAKI SPAM® is placed on a rectangle of cooked rice and wrapped in nori.

Nairagi: Japanese word for striped marlin. Called A'U in Hawaiian. Substitute any BILLFISH.

Nori: Japanese word for paper-thin sheets of seasoned, dried seaweed used for SUSHI. Available in Asian sections of supermarkets or in Asian markets.

Octopus: See TAKO.

Ogo: Japanese name for Gracilaria seaweed. Several Hawai'i aquaculture operations grow ogo, and it is widely available. Substitute finely julienned crisp CUCUMBER plus bits of dried NORI seaweed, or try rinsed sweet or dill pickles.

'Oka: Samoan term for Polynesian-style CEVICHE. Raw fish marinated in citrus juice and COCONUT MILK. "I'a 'ota" in writing or formal speech.

Onaga: Japanese name for red snapper. The Hawaiian name is 'ula'ula. Red snapper has pink flesh. Substitute any pink or red snapper, such as 'ŌPAKAPAKA.

Ono: Hawaiian name for a large mackerel, also known in Hawai'i as wahoo. Flesh has a white flaky texture. Substitute MAHIMAHI, halibut, cod, kingfish, swordfish.

'Ono: Hawaiian word for "delicious." Widely used in the Islands, even by non-Hawaiian speakers. Note the small mark at the start of the word; that's a glottal stop, an 'okina. ONO and 'ono are not the same word.

'Onolicious: Hawaiian slang for "tasty," combining the words "'ONO" and "delicious."

'Ōpae: Hawaiian freshwater SHRIMP. There are several varieties. Substitute small dried shrimp.

'Ōpakapaka: Hawaiian name for pink snapper. Has firm, light-pink flesh. Substitute any snapper.

'Opihi: Hawaiian and local term for several varieties of endemic limpets. They are found on rocky shores with strong wave action and are dangerous to gather. Substitute any edible limpet.

Oyster sauce: A thick brown sauce made from OYSTERS, brine, and SHOYU. Used in many stir-fried dishes. Substitute regular or vegetarian forms.

Oysters: Bivalve mollusks with thick, rough, irregular grayish or brownish shells. The top shell is larger and flatter than the lower one. Do not buy fresh unshelled oysters unless they are alive and full of water.

Panko: Japanese coarse breadcrumbs used for crunchy deep-fried coatings. Substitute fine dry breadcrumbs.

Papaya: A creamy tropical fruit with yellow or orange flesh and a shiny green or yellow skin. Substitute crenshaw melon to give similar color and texture (but not same flavor).

Peanut oil: A clear oil pressed from peanuts. Because of its high smoke point, it is prized for frying and deep-frying. Substitute grape seed oil.

Persian cucumber: See CUCUMBER.

Pesto: A paste made of fresh BASIL leaves, GARLIC, and pine nuts. Used to flavor pasta, fish, or meat dishes.

Pineapple: The fruit of a bromeliad plant originally native to Brazil. Its edible pulp is actually formed of multiple fruits fused into a compound. The yellowish flesh is fibrous, sweet, and juicy. It is sweeter and more tender near the base of the fruit. Available year-round in Hawai'i markets. Substitute fresh or canned.

Poi: A paste made from steamed, pounded TARO. Substitute unseasoned mashed potatoes thinned to a thick batter consistency.

Poisson cru: Traditional Tahitian CEVICHE made with lime juice and COCONUT MILK. Poisson cru means "raw fish" in French.

Poke: Hawaiian word for slice; refers to a traditional Hawaiian dish of sliced raw seafood.

Puhole: Edible fern shoots known on Maui as pohole and on other islands as hō'i'o. Native to Hawai'i, they are a deep-green fern with large fronds and green shoots that unfurl from the coiled head of the fern. The shoots have a slightly crunchy texture and sweet, buttery flavor. They are high in iron with calcium and magnesium. These ferns are edible and may be eaten fresh or cooked. Break off the bottom end like asparagus, then blanch to preserve their color. Rinse lightly in water to remove any fine hairs on the fern. Store in a dry container with a damp cloth and refrigerate. They should stay fresh up to a week.

Pūpū: Hawaiian and pidgin word for appetizer.

Radicchio: A red-leafed Italian chicory most often used as a salad green. When buying, look for leaves that are tender but firm, with a slightly bitter flavor. Substitute any chicory.

Rakkyo: Japanese name for a type of pickled onion. Substitute pickled onions.

Red cabbage: The red variety of regular "head" cabbage. Generally used in slaws. Substitute Napa cabbage (WON BOK).

Red chili pepper flakes: Dried and crushed red chili peppers. Found in the spice sections of most supermarkets. Substitute any chili pepper, finely chopped and seeded.

Red onion: Also known as purple onion. Sold in most produce sections in supermarkets. Widely used in salads.

Red snapper: See ONAGA.

Rice wine vinegar: Japan's relatively mild rice wine vinegar is the type most often found in local supermarkets. Chinese rice wine vinegars—white, red, and black—have a stronger flavor. Substitute a slightly sweetened light-colored vinegar.

Rock lobster: Also called spiny lobster. All the meat is in the tail. Rock lobsters have no claws. Available at the fishmarkets or in supermarkets. Sold fresh or frozen. Substitute any LOBSTER meat.

Sake: Slightly sweet Japanese rice wine. Substitute SHERRY.

Sambal oelek: A fiery-hot CHILI PASTE. A table condiment in Indonesia. Also known as hot Asian chili paste. Substitute any fiery-hot chili paste.

Sashimi: Very thin slices of fresh raw fish; a traditional Japanese appetizer. Substitute frozen scallops.

Scallops: Marine bivalve mollusks. The hinged muscle is sold canned, frozen, or fresh (unshelled). Many varieties of scallops are found in the world's waters. Scallops are generally classified as bay scallops (living in bays or estuaries) and sea scallops (living in the deep ocean).

Sesame oil: A dense, flavorful oil used as seasoning over much of East and South Asia. It is pressed from SESAME SEEDS. If cold-pressed from untoasted seeds, it will be very clear and mild-flavored. If pressed from toasted sesame seeds, it will be dark brown and strong-flavored.

Sesame seeds: The seeds of a flowering plant found throughout Eurasia and Africa; they have a distinctive nutty flavor. Different varieties of sesame produce different-colored seeds; some are white, some are black. They are sold unhulled or hulled, raw or toasted. The Japanese word for sesame is "goma." Substitute finely chopped toasted almonds.

Seven-spice seasoning: Also known as shichimi togarashi. Substitute mixture of ground chili peppers, black pepper, dried orange peel, SESAME SEEDS, poppy seeds, hemp seeds, and dried NORI seaweed.

Shallots: More like a GARLIC than an onion, with a head composed of one or two cloves. Has a mild onion flavor. Sold in most supermarkets. Substitute green onion bulb.

Sherry: A fortified Spanish wine, amber in color; sold dry, medium-dry, or sweet. Used for drinking or cooking.

Shichimi togarashi: See SEVEN-SPICE SEASONING.

Shiitake mushrooms: A variety of MUSHROOM cultivated in Japan and Korea. These dense, dark mushrooms are usually dried, then soaked to moisten before using. They have a meaty flavor.

Shirogoma: Japanese for white (hulled) SESAME SEEDS.

Shisho: An annual herb valued for its refreshing taste. Called shiso in Japanese, and widely used in Japanese cooking. It is best-known as shiso in the Islands. Shisho leaves are sometimes called beefsteak leaves (not related to the BEEFSTEAK TOMATO). There are several species of shisho; they are all members of the genus *Perilla*, which is a member of the mint family. Substitute mint or basil.

Shoyu: A salty liquid made from fermented boiled soybeans, roasted barley or wheat, monosodium glutamate (MSG), and salt. Usually dark brown in color, it is the principal seasoning in many styles of Asian cooking. There are many varieties of shoyu. Shoyu is the Japanese term, but it has been adopted into Island pidgin as the generic term for what is called SOY SAUCE on the Mainland. Substitute 3 parts Worcestershire sauce to 1 part water.

Shrimp: Swimming decapod crustaceans. There are many varieties found in all the world's waters, both saltwater and fresh. Many varieties are edible. Some edible shrimp are wild-caught, others are raised by aquaculturists. Biologists distinguish between shrimp and prawns, but in common speech, the terms are often used interchangeably. Americans tend to call all decapods shrimp, whereas speakers of British and Australian English are more apt to use the word "prawn."

Shutome: Japanese name for SWORDFISH. Substitute BILLFISH.

Soba noodles: Japanese thin buckwheat noodles. Substitute angel hair pasta.

Somen noodles: Delicate Japanese noodles made from hard wheat flour. Substitute vermicelli.

Soy sauce: See SHOYU. Shoyu is the term most frequently used in the Islands; soy sauce is more common on the U.S. Mainland.

SPAM®: A spiced luncheon meat sold in cans. Hawai'i residents developed a taste for SPAM® during World War II and have never lost it. SPAM® is used to make the ubiquitous SPAM® MUSUBI. Substitute ham.

Spiny lobster: See ROCK LOBSTER and LOBSTER. Use any lobster.

Squid: Squids and octopuses (TAKO) are both cephalopods. There are many varieties of squid, found in waters all over the world. Squid, fresh or frozen, is available in many supermarkets. When buying fresh squid, look for squid that are small and whole, with clear eyes and an ocean (but not fishy) smell. Squid must be carefully cooked so it does not become rubbery. Squid is frequently sold as CALAMARI. Substitute octopus.

Sriracha hot sauce: A proprietary hot sauce made from sun-ripened chili peppers, vinegar, GARLIC, sugar, and salt. It is made in the U.S., but is based on the hot sauces of Vietnam and Thailand.

Sushi: Japanese word for various foods made rice coated in a vinegar-sugar mixture. The rice is served with raw or poached seafood, vegetables, sliced omelet, and other tasty morsels. Some forms of sushi are wrapped in NORI.

Sweet onion: Any sweet, mild-flavored onion. Available in supermarket produce sections. (Examples: MAUI ONION, Vidalia onion, Walla Walla onion, Oso sweet onion, Rio sweet.)

Sweet potato: The orange-colored edible root of a tropical American vine. Often confused with the yam, which is starchier and less flavorful but can be used as a substitute.

Swordfish: A large marine game fish; also called broadbill. Substitute A'U (marlin) or other firm-fleshed white-meat fish. See also BILLFISH.

Tako: Japanese word for octopus. In daily speech, Islanders tend to say "tako" or HE'E rather than "octopus." Tako is a cephalopod and is related to the SQUID. There are about 300 known varieties of tako; humans eat many of them. Tako can be difficult to cook, as it can become rubbery if not handled correctly. It should not be over-cooked. It is sometimes tenderized. This is a controversial subject, as there are many competing theories as to the best way to tenderize tako. Some say that it does not need tenderizing if it is correctly cooked. Substitute squid.

Taro: A nutritious, starchy tuber used for making POI, the traditional Hawaiian staple. More than 200 taro varieties are grown worldwide. It cannot be eaten raw, as raw taro is full of irritating oxalic acid crystals. These crystals dissolve when the taro is boiled or steamed. Substitute any firm-fleshed potato, such as red potatoes or new potatoes.

Tartare: Finely chopped raw meat or fish, usually served with seasoning or sauce. Originally a European dish.

Temaki sushi: SUSHI rice and accompaniments rolled into a NORI cone.

Teriyaki: Japanese word for a marinade or sauce for meat or fish, generally consisting of SHOYU, sugar, GINGER, and GARLIC. Substitute mixture of shoyu, SAKE or SHERRY, sugar, and ginger.

Thai basil: A variety of BASIL grown in Thailand. Substitute sweet basil.

Thai chilies: Also called bird's-eye chilies. These chilies are very small and fiery-hot; often sold dried. Can be used in place of HAWAIIAN CHILIES.

Thyme: Cooks use the leaves from this aromatic herb native to the Mediterranean region. Sold fresh in supermarket produce sections or dried, in the spice section.

Ti leaves: The leaves of a woody plant in the agave family. Grown throughout Polynesia. Used to wrap foods before cooking them in an earth oven (see IMU). Substitute BANANA LEAVES, corn husks, or aluminum foil.

Tobiko: Flying fish roe. Substitute any fish roe.

Tofu: Japanese name for a bland-flavored soybean curd that can be custard-like in texture (soft tofu) or quite firm. The firm or extra-firm forms are generally used in stir-frying or deep-frying.

Tombo: Japanese word for albacore tuna. Substitute any tuna.

Tsume: A sweet glaze or sauce used in Japanese cooking. Usually made from SHOYU, MIRIN, sugar, and fish or shellfish broth.

Uku: Hawaiian name for the gray snapper.

Ulua: Hawaiian word for jackfish; it refers to eleven different species of jackfish. It includes the GIANT TREVALLY. Substitute any crevalle, jack, or pompano game fish.

Uni: Sea urchin roe.

Wasabi: Hot green Japanese horseradish. Pungent root with an extremely strong, sharp flavor. Popular Japanese condiment. Available in most Hawai'i supermarkets. Substitute hot dry mustard.

White miso: Fermented soybean paste containing rice.

White pepper: Made from pepper berries picked when very ripe and completely red. They are soaked in salt water for a few days to dissolve the outer shell, exposing the white inner seed. The peppercorns are then dried. Their flavor is much milder than that of black peppercorns. Substitute black pepper.

Wild rice: Also called "Indian rice." A long-grain marsh grass native to the Great Lakes area of the United States. Known for its nutty flavor and chewy texture. Available in supermarkets.

Wok: A versatile round-bottomed pan used in Chinese cookery; used with and without a cover for stir-frying, steaming, boiling, braising, and deep-frying. A similar dish, the karhai, is used in India.

Won bok: Chinese cabbage or Napa cabbage. Substitute savoy cabbage or other green cabbage.

Wonton wrappers: Also called egg-roll skins or spring-roll wrappers. Flat, thin squares of wheat dough, used to wrap various tasty fillings. Available in Asian markets. Can be bought fresh or frozen. Keep refrigerated.

Index

Tobiko, 40, 45, 47, 92, 97, 108-111, 131, 152
Tofu, 27, 49, 87, 89, 144

U

Uhu, 106-107

W

Wahoo, 23, 45, 65
Wasabi, 39-40, 45, 90, 92, 97, 102, 108-109, 130-131, 138
Wonton strips, 83, 103
Yukke Sauce, 110-111

About Sam Choy

Chef Sam Choy has been creating cuisine with fresh, local island ingredients since he was a boy learning to cook alongside his parents. His culinary creativity led him to co-create and popularize Hawai'i Regional Cuisine around the globe.

Before the words "Farm-to-Table" ever came together, sourcing and cooking with the traditional foods of Hawai'i was a way of life for Sam. His 'Kai Lanai' restaurant in Keahou, Kona is partnered with local farmers, ranchers, and fisherman to bring Hawai'i Island's freshest and sustainably raised food to the table. These local ingredients provide the base for Sam's unique Hawaiian fusion cooking style. In recognition of his artistry and commitment to using fresh and sustainable ingredients, Choy is a featured chef at the annual *Cooking for Solutions* event at the Monterey Bay Aquarium.

Sam Choy is as comfortable in front of a camera as he is in the kitchen. He has appeared on numerous Food Network shows including *Chopped: Grill Masters, Iron Chef America* and *East Meets West with Ming Tsai.* He has been a guest star twice on *Hawaii Five-O,* appearing with Iron Chef Masaharu Morimoto and Carol Burnett.

Sam brings his Hawaiian-fresh cooking to significant events for some of the world's most influential companies including Google and the annual "Big Damn Luau" at Facebook. (He brings his big heart to the table for causes that are important to him—the UH Seidman Cancer Center, *St. Croix Food and Wine Experience* benefitting the St. Croix Foundation, *L.A. Food and Wine* benefitting No Kid Hungry and Berkley Foundation and *Wine to Water* benefitting Water Hope in Napa, California. Sam also cooks for U.S. Military men and women on bases all over the world.)

Sam is the author of eighteen cookbooks, sixteen with Mutual Publishing and two with Hyperion. In 2004, Sam was awarded the James Beard Foundation Award America's Classic Award for Sam Choy's Koloko in Kailua-Kona, on the

Big Island of Hawai'i. The award recognizes "beloved regional restaurants" that reflect the character of their communities.

Sam is known for making poke mainstream and a household word in the Islands. It started in 1991, when he and his friend Gene Erger sponsored Hawai'i's first poke contest on the Big Island. The improvised contest was so popular that it returned the next year and went on to becoming an annual event in larger venues. Contestants looking for an edge soon moved beyond the standard 'ahi-green onion-shoyu-sesame oil poke and created increasingly elaborate dishes. The contest is now held on O'ahu.

Cooking and enjoying good food is a way of life for Sam Choy that grew out of the land and sea of his home in Hawai'i. Wherever he is in the world, Sam brings his aloha spirit and unique Hawaiian fusion flavors.